BIG BROTHER
IS LISTENING

the last date stamped before

BIG BROTHER IS LISTENING

Phonetappers & the security state

DUNCAN CAMPBELL

Reports from the *New Statesman,*
first published between February 1979 and July 1980;
updated in January 1981.

NS
Report 2

DUNCAN CAMPBELL has been a New Statesman staff writer since 1978. In 1977 he was prosecuted with another journalist for contravening the Official Secrets Act by interviewing a former soldier. The 'ABC' case arose out of investigations he and others had carried out into the dangers to liberty posed by Britain's burgeoning intelligence bureaucracy. The case was unsuccessful for the government and brought to light many unacceptable security activities — such as jury vetting — for the first time.

Since then he has specialised in investigative reporting for the New Statesman, and besides the reports contained here, has unearthed many unpleasant, corrupt and repressive aspects of secret government activity.

CONTENTS

ACKNOWLEDGEMENT

Cover photographs by Duncan Campbell and Chris Davies

Typeset & designed by
Redesign, 7a Duncan Terrace, London N1.

Printed by
Manchester Free Press, 59 Whitworth Street, Manchester 1.

Published by
New Statesman, 10 Great Turnstile, London WC1.

ISBN 0 900962 08 9

Trade distribution by
Scottish & Northern Book Distribution Ltd.
18 Granby Row, Manchester 1.
&
45/47 Niddry Street, Edinburgh 1.

Southern Distribution
27 Clerkenwell Close, London EC1.

CHAPTER ONE

The Threat of the Electronic Spies

Oversight of the burgeoning international security and intelligence *apparat* is a considerable problem for democracy. Vast sums are swallowed on intelligence collection, yet the agencies systematically fail to foresee important crises. There is a clear case for public and parliamentary scrutiny.

The unveiling of 'Sigint'

In the course of the 'ABC' trial at the Old Bailey in 1978, it was officially confirmed that two massive buildings in Cheltenham, Gloucestershire, are the offices of Government Communications Headquarters (GCHQ); that the work of this organisation involves signals intelligence (Sigint), now officially defined as the 'reception and analysis of foreign communications and other electronic transmissions for intelligence purposes'; and that it is a 'majority shareholder in British intelligence'

For some reason, GCHQ has never attracted the same degree of public interest as other intelligence agencies – perhaps because its image is less glamorous than that of the Special Branch or M16, or because its work (as officially defined) sounds relatively harmless. In fact, it is larger and potentially far more sinister, its influence more widespread, and the implications of its work ultimately more threatening to civil liberty and world peace, than all the other agencies put together. It deserves the closest scrutiny by the public, yet it resists this with all its might.

Signals intelligence is not a new idea. It is founded, after all, on the ancient and dishonourable tradition of governments reading other people's mail. GCHQ's direct roots go back at least as far as the Foreign Office 'black chambers' of the 1920s, but well before that code breakers and monitors of communications had become deeply imbued with the idea that their work must be kept secret at all costs. Secrecy remains a vital and

integral part of GCHQ's work today. Every one of tens of thousands of
military and civilian personnel working in Sigint is subject to intensive
'indocrination' every time they move to a new post. As they leave, they must
be 'de-indoctrinated' and reminded of an obligation never to disclose any
information whatsoever to 'anyone not currently indoctrinated'. At each
stage, a long lecture is delivered on the importance of the work and the need
for secrecy.

It was not until 1974 that a corner of the veil was lifted. After a
lengthy battle with the authorities, Group Captain Winterbotham of M16
(who was, ironically, one of the early protagonists of 'indoctrination')
managed to publish his memoirs of wartime codebreaking in a book called
The Ultra Secret. Winterbotham was no whistle blower; he merely believed
that such a glorious episode in the nation's history (and one which shed a
fine light upon himself) should not go unrecorded. Once he had broken the
ice, a gaggle of wartime practitioners emerged from the wings to tell their
stories. From private research, and from these books and others published
abroad, it is possible to piece together a picture of Sigint operations which is
not only highly alarming, but also a great deal more detailed than those
involved would like it to be.

GCHQ is a partner in a multinational 'Sigint pact', whose task is to
monitor the entire globe. The basic instrument of unity is a series of agreements
signed between the United States and the UK around 1947 (known as the
UKUSA pact), which Canada, Australia and New Zealand later joined.
The pact is hierarchical: at the top is the US National Security Agency
(NSA), which has its headquarters at Fort George C. Meade in Maryland.
GCHQ has the status of a senior partner, while Canada, Australia and New
Zealand are 'second parties'. 'Third parties' include the NATO allies,
notably Germany and Norway. France and Sweden are also participants
and links have existed with Finland, South Africa and Brazil, among
others.

Each of the main participants – NSA, GCHQ, Australia's Defence
Signals Division (DSD) and Canada's Communications Branch of the
National Research Council (CBNRC) — is in charge of Sigint activities in a
given region. GCHQ's territory is Africa and Europe east of the Ural
mountains. Technical liaison between the participants is, of necessity, close
and well integrated. They share procedures for identifying and labelling
signals and have a unified communications network. Voluminous 'International Regulations on Sigint' – IRSIG for short – prescribe security
procedures, including indoctrination, to which participating governments
must agree. They share, too, outlandish codewords such as VIPAR,
TRINE or UMBRA, which must always designate Top Secret Sigint
material. Everything that is intercepted is sent to Fort Meade, and generally
also to Cheltenham as well as to other concerned stations around the world.

Ears around the globe
The scale of international communications has increased enormously over

Steadman

the last 30 years and the Sigint agencies have swollen to a corresponding size. NSA employs more than 120,000 people in different parts of the world. The size of GCHQ is – of course – supposed to be a secret, but it is possible to estimate the scale of operations by looking at the better-known bases. The two office blocks in Cheltenham have ample room for between four and five thousand employees. One thousand personnel or so are employed in each of the major monitoring bases, army centres in Cyprus and West Germany, RAF units in Lincolnshire and West Berlin, and civilian units in Staffordshire, Devon, Cornwall and Hong Kong. Then there are smaller units scattered around Britain and in Malta, Mauritius, Turkey, Iran, Ascension Island and Australia, with further detachments elsewhere. So the total number of GCHQ related staff may be more than 20,000.

Another indicator of its size is that, while GCHQ is listed rather modestly as the 'Signals Department' of the Foreign Office, its director is a Deputy Secretary and it has five or six Under Secretaries. The entire remaining Foreign Office establishment is not many times larger.

Although nominally responsible to the Foreign Secretary, GCHQ's actual lines of command may fall somewhere between the Cabinet Office (where a Co-ordinator of Intelligence and Security looks after the work of all secret agencies) and Fort Meade. Chapman Pincher's recent comment is probably accurate:

> Dependence is so great (of GCHQ) upon NSA) and co-operation so close that I am convinced security chiefs would go to any lengths to protect the link-up . . .'

NSA has five major independent establishments in Britain: Chicksands, Bedfordshire (telephone and telex monitoring, and control of SIGINT satellites); Edzell, Scotland (radio monitoring); Menwith Hill, Harrogate; Mildenhall, Suffolk (SIGINT and spy aircraft), and SUSLO, Grosvenor Square, London (communications centre). Their activities are similarly shrouded in secrecy.

Sigint work involves a great deal more than interception of telecommunications from bases on the ground. 'Provocative' missions into foreign air and sea space are a regular feature. Since 1945, more than 70 US aircraft have been destroyed on missions of this kind – and ship casualties have been high, too. The Tonkin Gulf incident, which the US used to justify the Vietnam war, was the result of an intrusion by the USS *Maddox,* engaged on work for NSA. When the USS *Liberty* was attacked by the Israelis off Gaza in 1967, it had been trying to monitor Israeli communications during the Six-Day War: more than 40 seamen and NSA personnel were killed and the ship was very nearly sunk. The most recent incident of this kind was the capture, intact, of the USS *Pueblo* while it was spying off the North Korean coast. And in addition, US nuclear submarines have several times collided with Soviet ships while engaged in the extraordinary 'Project Holystone', spying in Soviet waters, even going as far as the entrance to Vladivostok harbour.

Britain has had its share of such international mischief. Two undergraduates were put on trial under the Official Secrets Act in 1958 for revealing details of espionage work in the Baltic and on one occasion as far afield as Leningrad, by British aircraft and small ships, often operating under the Swedish flag. Two RAF aircraft were reported lost on a 'provocative' mission over the Caspian Sea in the early 1960s. Nowadays, two enormously expensive, specially equipped Nimrod aircraft are sent from their base in East Anglia on regular monitoring flights along the east European border. Large trawlers which spend long periods in northern waters sometimes carry naval staff equipped with interception receivers. Trawlers such as the *Gaul,* which was mysteriously lost in the Norwegian Sea three years ago, may do this work.

Spying on allies
Although it is piously denied, spying on allies is an accepted rule in the Sigint game. For example, ex-employees of NSA at Chicksands have reported that the base monitors French diplomatic traffic. They have also

alleged that it monitors British government and commercial communications – and similar allegations have been made in Parliament. British bases in Germany and Cyprus monitor NATO allies. During the early stages of negotiations to join the Common Market, GCHQ was reportedly required to decipher a considerable amount of diplomatic traffic passing between our prospective European partners, and for this purpose it drew heavily on NSA's resources. At the time of the Suez crisis, the Americans intercepted diplomatic and military telegrams of the British and French governments and used the information to frustrate their strategies. This caused so much antagonism – and the only known rift in the Sigint pact – that in 1957 the prominent US cryptographer William Friedman was sent on an NSA special mission to GCHQ to restore relations and study advances in cryptography that had been made in Britain, Sweden and Switzerland. (Two years ago, NSA fought to prevent publication of details of Friedman's trip, on the grounds that it might deprive NSA of its ability to read the coded messages of all NATO countries.)

Sigint has also turned its attentions to individual citizens. In 1975 the Church Committee of the US Senate uncovered NSA programmes to intercept the international telephone and telex messages of targeted American citizens. These programmes, known as SHAMROCK and MINARET, included the interception of all telephone and telegraph traffic to or from the United States. Other intelligence agencies provided 'watch lists' to NSA. Be 1974 there were extensive files on 75,000 people, and Bob Woodward (of Watergate fame) revealed in the *Washington Post* in 1975 that NSA had intercepted the messages of such anti-war dissidents as Jane Fonda and Benjamin Spock.

GCHQ has its own version of SHAMROCK and MINARET. The famous 'D-Notice Affair' of 1967 centred on the (relatively trivial) relevation that all overseas Post Office telegrams were collected and read by security officials. In 1977, the president of Western Union International told the US senate that the British government had demanded copies of all overseas telegrams handled by the company since 1945. Interception of most UK overseas telephone traffic is carried out not by GCHQ, but by NSA at its Menwith Hill site, near Harrogate (as detailed later on in this report). A station of the Composite Signals Organisation (the civilian monitoring agency run by GCHQ) is located congenially in Earls Court, high in a Ministry of Defence tower block at the back of the exhibition hall, and monitors radio and telephone traffic in the London area, including, presumably, foreign embassies.

Operations of this kind are mainly illegal. Interception of diplomatic communications, of whatever kind, is contrary to British and international law – and in particular, it contravenes the Diplomatic Privileges Act of 1964, which ratified the Vienna Convention on Diplomatic Relations. The International Telecommunications Convention, ratified by the British government, places a general duty on signatories to preserve the secrecy of international communications (although it allows a little leeway). Trainees for GCHQ are left in no doubt about this point, and are instructed that the technical illegality is an important reason why the public should not know of their work.

An alternative, secret history

The secrecy which surrounds the work of GCHQ and other Sigint agencies affords considerable power to those who control it. In particular, they have propagated an alternative, secret, version of history, known only to a privileged and powerful few, which cannot easily be challenged by anyone else. After the Second World War, it was determined that no access to so-called 'special intelligence' material should be permitted to official historians, and that such chronicling as was necessary would be undertaken by 'indoctrinated personnel'. A 'concordat' to this effect was apparently signed between the British cabinet and President Truman in 1946 – the harbinger of more extensive agreements extant today.

For 30 years then, there existed in the minds of the indoctrinated a version of history which looked very different from that officially described. The practitioners of the secret world were able to present those in government with an unchallengeable account of how intelligence in general and Sigint in particular had played an essential part in winning the war and would continue to be indispensable in the future. This singular world view only started to open up with the publication of Winterbotham's book, *The Ultra Secret*. Since then, independent historians have begun to examine the achievements of The Government Code and Cypher School at Bletchley, and have come to the conclusion that, despite claims to the contrary, it did not singlehandedly win World War Two. At certain critical moments (such as the Battle of Britain), intelligence was irregular or unavailable – or even unusable because of a lack of defensive resources. For at least half the war, poor British codes and cyphers probably gave away as much as was gained. Even the mathematical achievements in codebreaking and intelligence are now being researched by independent historians, and may eventually seem mundane, rather than the work of genius.

To preserve the co-operation of government, the secret world operates a successful carrot-and-stick strategy. The carrot is admission to a very exclusive club where members are allowed to know about top secret matters which, because they are known only inside the charmed circle, appear to be highly significant. The stick is the carefully cultivated fear that the national interest would be threatened if the strictest secrecy were not maintained.

It is easy to see how effectively this cult of secrecy serves the interests of GCHQ and its allies. Members of Parliament and even junior ministers in defence and the Foreign Office are excluded from the club; if they ask awkward questions, they are told it would not be 'in the national interest' for them to have the answers. Advisers to one major government department which could usefully use Sigint information on commodity prices have said that 'none of that kind of information ever reaches us'. According to Chapman Pincher, Jim Callaghan is sent 'important intercepts by GCHQ

(GCHQ photograph)

Left: GCHQ's crest bombastically gives the game away. Its title, signals flashes symbolising Sigint, and the accolade of a laurel wreath, surround the globe. Above: one of the two large Cheltenham offices housing the largest intelligence organisation in Britain. Below: the NSA base at Chicksands, Bedfordshire.

(USAF photograph)

... daily in oblong yellow boxes'. But even he, says Pincher, is 'treated on a "need to know" basis'. GCHQ, not the Prime Minister, decides which bits of information he gets. Richard Hall explains in his book on GCHQ's Australian partner, *The Secret State,* that a common Sigint tactic is to keep ministers happy by feeding them with distracting low grade information. When Sigint finds a 'diplomatic titbit with the minister's name in it' says Hall, 'these are almost always pushed forward'.

Shaping foreign policy

Foreign policy is often shaped, secretly, by Sigint. GCHQ's close links with the NSA are a major ingredient in the cement which seals Britain's dependent alliance with the United States. The NSA, in turn, can secretly shape US foreign policy. For example, it purchased the right to maintain an enormous base at Asmara in Ethiopia by sending millions of dollars' worth of military and economic assistance to Haile Selassie. The US Congress remained unaware that the bases existed or that the payments had been made. Similar arrangements were made for setting up three stations in Morocco. When Allende came to power in Chile, the NSA rapidly had to dismantle a major installation on Easter Island – which must have been an important spur to the decision to 'destabilise' the new Socialist government. The network of surveillance bases in Turkey, monitoring the Soviet Union, has for a long time been a key factor in US-Turkish relations: at one stage it forced the US to withdraw the pressure on the Turkish government to clamp down on heroin production.

Britain has similar secret commitments. Foreign policy towards Cyprus has been determined largely by the fact that it is the site of major Sigint and other surveillance activity. A GCHQ station in Iran – run in co-operation with the notorious Iranian secret police, Savak, was among the clutch of spying stations which had to close down urgently after the 1979 revolution. Its existence was a secret factor determining Britain's attitude to developments in Iran. According to openly available circulars, GCHQ employees were working regularly in South Africa at least as recently as 1970. Britain has a major interest in one of the Turkish stations, Sinop, on the Black Sea: British technicians working there for GCHQ and under GCHQ contracts with Cable and Wireless Ltd, were killed in a terrorist attack in 1972.

By monopolising information, Sigint agencies have made it virtually impossible for governments to control them. One episode which illustrates this with frightening clarity is the sacking of Gough Whitlam, the Australian Prime Minister. Whitlam had made himself very unpopular with the intelligence community by asking questions about Pine Gap, a station run by the NSA. He had also caused a secret base in Singapore to be closed by identifying it publicly; and his Attorney General had led a raid by armed police to recover information being witheld from the government by the Australian Secret Intelligence Organisation (Australia's M15). In the end, the CIA sent a telegram to Australian intelligence which declared that if 'this problem' could not be 'solved', it could not 'see how our mutually beneficial relationships are going to continue.' The problem was promptly solved when the Governor General suddenly chose to relieve Whitlam of his post.

It is difficult for obvious reasons to find out whether similar battles are waged behind Whitehall's lace curtains. We know, at least, about the bugging of Harold Wilson's offices at Downing Street and in the House of Commons, revealed in 1978. This was done not by M15 but by a special electronics unit run by GCHQ, according to Chapman Pincher. James Callaghan denied the allegation, but of course the first credential of any such undercover activity is that it can be denied at the highest level. GCHQ is responsible for providing the Prime Minister with secure communications and protection from bugging by the 'enemy': it therefore has perfect access, should it want to do any monitoring itself. When Callaghan made his denial, his brief was prepared by the then co-ordinator of intelligence in the Cabinet Office, Sir Leonard Hooper. Sir Leonard is a former director of GCHQ, where he had worked for 32 years.

Not only has Sigint phenomenally increased the extent of its activities since the war; it has also changed in character. Its priorities have shifted away from urgently needed military intelligence and technological innovations have made some tasks impossible. For instance, the major codes of the Soviet Union are now, like those of the US and the UK, largely uncrackable and even analysis of traffic levels (the varying volume of communications) can be unrevealing. Former CIA director William Colby admitted to the Church Committee that most of NSA's major successes have been obtained not by diligent technical breakthroughs, but by the theft of codebooks and 'keys' from embassies around the world: the same is presumably true of GCHQ.

The sheer volume of information can inhibit Sigint's effectiveness, as the Pike Committee of the US House of Representatives recognised in January 1976. Commenting on the failure of the intelligence community to predict the 1975 Middle East war, the Committee said: 'NSA intercepts of Egyptian-Syrian war preparations were so voluminous – hundreds of reports each week – that few analysts had time to digest more than a small portion. Costly intercepts had scant impact on intelligence estimates.' Some of the more highly classified material took so long to be distributed that the war had broken out before the relevant messages were read. Similar difficulties have attended other events in the Middle East and Eastern Mediterranean.

Amid mounting technical obstacles, Sigint has shifted its aim towards weaker targets: third world governments, dissident civilian nationals, economic intelligence and low grade communications from the major powers. In *The Secret State,* Richard Hall reproduced a 1975 Sigint report on world oil prices: it was portentously marked with the required international designations (CODEWORD material . . . TOP SECRET

UMBRA), but the information it contained could easily have been lifted from the pages of the *Financial Times*.

Costly and un-accountable

The cost of Sigint is enormous. GCHQ's total annual budget must be well over £200m — which makes public accountability imperative. Why does GCHQ maintain a costly post in Hong Kong? What is its importance to current British strategy? Does it bring in useful exchange commodities from the United States? If so, what are these, and what exactly does the small print of the deal say? Is this the best way to allocate scarce resources? If £200m is committed to defence, would it perhaps be better spent – at least in part – on tanks or front line aircraft?

In view of the enormous budget, there is also a case for concern about commercial companies' involvement with GCHQ. Racal enjoys a particularly favoured relationship among communications manufacturers. Large orders for a basic Sigint surveillance receiver, the Racal RA17, were placed in the late 1950s at a critical time in the company's development. A special subsidiary was set up to make surveillance equipment for GCHQ; its managers and salesmen include former GCHQ and MoD civil servants.

The secret world maintains that it cannot make itself in any way publicly accountable because that would threaten the 'national interest'. But details of the Sigint pact have been well known internationally since 1960. That was the year in which two NSA defectors revealed at a Moscow press conference a full account of GCHQ-NSA link up and its ramifications. For good measure, they produced a list of some of the 40 countries whose codes NSA was then successfully cracking. Some changed their codes as a result, but many did not – perhaps because they felt they had too much invested in the current code, or because they took the view that nothing was hurt except their pride as long as only the major powers were reading their messages, not their neighbours.

GCHQ has had its own defectors, but has kept silent about them. There have been at least two. An Intelligence Corps corporal working in Sigint at the 13th Signals Regiment in West Berlin crossed the Berlin Wall in July 1963 and stayed in East Germany; and in September 1968, a Chief Technician working at the RAF Sigint centre in Digby, Lincolnshire was arrested after passing secret information to Soviet agents. One of his offences, for which he is still in prison, was revealing that GCHQ had followed Soviet radio call signs for more than 20 years, using captured wartime documents.

The Sigint community clings to secrecy because its power depends upon it. The arguments it uses in self-justification were well aired at the Official Secrets trial in 1978: allies must be spied upon because one day they might become enemies; countries which seem remote now must nevertheless be monitored because they might one day become part of a larger conflict; information about signals intelligence and cryptography must be tightly restricted so as not to alert targets to the dangers of interception; true, some countries know they are being monitored, but it is essential they should not know the level of sophistication of the monitoring.

The fundamental effect of this policy is to inhibit any scientific advance which is not directly controlled by the indoctrinated. They are threatened at present by two developments: by the introduction of micro-electronics which can make even expensive cyphering systems uncrackable except through disproportionate effort; and by a new form of cypher system which removes the need for secret distribution of code 'keys', thus opening the door to much wider public use of secret communication. Even in the early days, NSA and GCHQ were determined to classify and restrict information which had previously been available, in order to establish a monopoly. Today, NSA and its partners are fighting a furious battle to control the blossoming public interest in cryptography. They have attempted to stop publication of scientific papers by independent researchers; they have tried to interfere in the allocation of grants. NSA has succeeded in having the first US publicly standardised cryptographic system adjusted to its specification – which probably means it can now crack it. Both NSA and GCHQ prohibit the export of cryptographic equipment unless the manufacturer hands over complete plans.

The UKUSA pact, with its goal of WASP global surveillance seems in retrospect to reflect a postwar design for US hegemony. Yet Sigint has maintained that goal and protected it from changing public opinion. Why? In the course of his investigations in the US Congress, Frank Church commented that NSA's technology 'at any time could be turned around on the American people . . . the capacity is there to make tyranny total'. If that is the direction in which NSA is heading, its Cheltenham poodles cannot be far behind.

First published 2 February 1979.

CHAPTER TWO

The Phone Tappers Exposed

(with Nick Anning)

The cover of this booklet portrays the man who runs a highly-secretive Post Office installation in Chelsea. This is the government's phone-tapping centre — the scope of its operations is much larger than Parliament has ever been told.

Chelsea home of 'Tinkerbell'

Britain's national telephone-tapping service operates from a building concealed behind the Industrial Tribunals Central Office at 93 Ebury Bridge Road, SW1, just opposite Chelsea Barracks. This is the organisation which is known in police lore as 'Tinkerbell'. Here thousands of telephone lines up and down the country are monitored every year, and the results supplied to the spy 'customers' – chiefly M15, Scotland Yard's Special Branch, and the C11 squad.

'Tinkerbell' can be identified in the first place simply because this large facility appears only in ghostly form in the Post Office's official records and directories. Most Post Office activities, naturally, are publicly listed in some detail, together with accounts of their work and the responsibilities of their staff. But 'Tinkerbell' appears only as the Equipment Development Division of the PO Operational Programming Department, OP5. Its address is given as Telecommunications Headquarters, in the City, but there are no facilities there except a dropping-point for mail. It also has a City phone number, 432 4132. Operations, however, clearly centre on the building at Ebury Bridge Road, which is sealed-off through a mews: there is a small plaque bearing the letters 'PO/THQ/OPD/EDD'.

The centre has been in use for almost ten years, and according to local planning records it is a 'computer centre'. Ordinary PO staff are not allowed into the centre, which has permanently-locked doors. Its windows, overlooked by a block of Peabody Trust flats, are covered by opaque white curtains, never parted. Observation shows that it is staffed 24 hours a day: local residents are accustomed to the lights burning all night, and to frequent

The national phone tapping centre at 93 Ebury Bridge Road, SW1.

security alarms. Shifts of workers – a good many of whom appear to be female telephone supervisors – come and go during the small hours.

The Post Office of course has facilities in many parts of the country, which are employed in developing new equipment of various kinds. They are for the most part publicly identified, and do not work around the clock. (Elsewhere, of course, the Post Office also has substantial and well-known computer centres.) 'Tinkerbell' appears to act as headquarters for the teams of selected PO engineers who visit telephone exchanges to instal taps. These men frequently travel in standard PO vans, which are said by other engineers to be something of a 'giveaway' since they are just labelled 'Post Office Telephones', and do not have the usual words saying which telephone Manager is responsible for them. Union officials have seen Post Office documents which suggest that at least 125 staff in the highly-paid Executive Engineering grades (equivalent to fairly senior-level administrative officers in the Civil Service) are employed in OP5. The recent hiving-off of British Telecommunications from the Post Office has not affected the tappers: they have merely changed their name from OP5 to ES4, and adopted a new title:

'Equipment Development Policy Division'. The secretive nature of OP5 is confirmed by the sparseness of its entry in the Post Office central staff directory — which normally runs to quite elaborate accounts of each official's function. Its Director — and by implication the chief phone-tapper — is Mr Philip R. F. Harris, who lives in St Albans. His predecessor, Mr. A. E. Harvey of Chislehurst, retired in 1980 with a CBE.

When we approached Mr Harris at his home, he would only confirm that he is employed by the Post Office. When it was put to him that he was in charge of phone-tapping, he refused to make any comment.

Cottage industry to big business

In addition to what can be deduced from Post Office records, from observation and from background knowledge about the 'state of the art' in telecommunications surveillance, there is some information available from employees and ex-employees of the Post Office (although it is unlikely that any will identify themselves, in the absence of a full-scale public inquiry). This helps to chart the rise of the phone-tapping business from something of a cottage industry in the fifties – when the last attempt was made at systematic scrutiny through the Birkett report – to the extensive, high-technology system which exists today.

An employee who has worked in the phone-tapping operation says that the Ebury Road system was planned during the late sixties. Facilities then being proposed would have the capacity to tap 1,000 lines simultaneously. We put this to ex-Inspector Dick Lee, who headed the Operation Julie drugs investigation, and used phone-tapping extensively in the work. He said the estimate 'doesn't surprise me – with the technology that's available'. He confirmed that all telephone tapping was centralised at a facility in London, which he has visited.

Interviews with ex-Post Office employees, crosschecked with accounts of police investigations, suggest that less than 100 of Tinkerbell's lines are available for police inquiries into serious crime, with the remainder being devoted to the secret services. To judge by Dick Lee's recollections, the facilities available to the police remain fairly cumbersome. Long hours of listening to tapes, and sorting out trivial from important traffic, can make the process very labour-intensive. In the past, the necessity of employing many people, fulltime, to sort out the calls made, for example, to relatives from the calls made to the shopsteward's committee has always been a restriction on the extent of phone-tapping.

Our inquiries suggest that some of the facilities available at Ebury Bridge Road – though not necessarily ones which are available to the police – go far beyond this difficulty. Computerised retrieval systems enable particular connections to be automatically logged, so that a 'target' subscriber's calls need only be transcribed when he or she makes a call to some destination likely to be interesting. It is also suggested that advanced machine-transcription systems are becoming available, so that results of phone-taps can be made swiftly and easily available to 'customers'. In

Left: Phil Harris, Head of the Post Office Equipment Development Division, which taps phones. Right: Brinley Jones, Controller of the Post Office Investigation Division, which opens mail.

short, centralisation and technological rationalisation drastically lowers the marginal cost of phone-tapping. The equipment at Ebury Bridge Road was designed by GCHQ, the government's code-and-cypher centre at Cheltenham. This has access to the latest US know-how, including computerised voice recognition techniques. According to one tapping centre employee, voice-recognition operations have reached an advanced stage – given the availability of good-quality lines – and by 1978 speech on many lines could be transcribed automatically and printed-out almost 'on demand'. The centre apparently has direct links to GCHQ, to M15 at Century House, through which recorded calls can be replayed on request.

There have been two major booms in phone-tapping in the last 20 years. The first came in the late fifties, when operations were centralised in London instead of being done ad-hoc through local exchanges. The major London centre was close to Vauxhall Bridge Road, SW1, behind the present M16 'London Station' at No. 60. That office had a capacity of 300 lines by the mid-sixties. Since there were three or four other centres in use, and the 1956 level of operation was described in the Birkett report of 1957 as no more than 159 taps *in an entire year,* a massive expansion had already taken place.

A training centre for tapping was established in an office in Petty France, SW1 (since demolished to make way for the new Home Office HQ). A small amount of police tapping was done there. By the late sixties, though, the obsolescence and incompatibility of some of the equipment produced a desire to bring new systems together under one roof: the result was Ebury Bridge Road.

A national network of tapping connections covers the entire country, with 12 lines at least usually connected to every 'group' exchange in major cities. To prevent ordinary Post Office engineers recognising this system and its purpose, the lines are included in the Defence Communications Network, which is installed for military communications. It runs through ordinary Post Office facilities, but details of its operations are secret.

The phone tappers are aware that they are not popular with the ordinary engineers. They normally attach their taps outside ofice hours, gaining access to exchanges with special keys. Sometimes their tapping connections — which are often recognisable to exchange engineers — have been removed by other staff. It is said that some years ago a tapper who was making an urgent connection to a union line during a strike found himself surrounded by exchange employees who regaled him with a chorus of *Land of Hope and Glory* (Mother of the Free!). There is no suggestion that warranted police taps, targeted against serious crime, have been interfered with.

Tapping the Grunwick strikers, and others
Roughly 90 people come to work each morning at Ebury Bridge Road. They include technicians and representatives of 'customer' departments. Many of the shift workers who operate the tapping services are women, and appear to be recruited from staff in 'Service Observations' – a more legitimate if objectionable system of random tapping which is designed to monitor and measure the normal workings of the phone system.

Calls reaching the centre from tapped lines are passed via a computer to multi-channel tape recorders and storage discs: one recorder can deal with 36 or more lines (perhaps up to 100), according to frequency of use. A central register of all telephone numbers in the country, together with the names and addresses, is available: together with computerised facilities for 'scanning' connections, a set-up of this kind can provide, cheaply and easily, surveillance-power on a scale Lord Birkett never dreamed of.

Military intelligence appears to be the only agency still running a separate centre (many Intelligence Corps personnel were trained in tapping techniques during the sixties, and operated on civilian telephones in Cyprus and in Germany). The Army now runs a listening post, comparable to the Chelsea installation, on the top floor of Churchill House, a Post Office building in Belfast: we have no specific information about any possible Army tapping operations on the mainland.

One Post Office engineer described to us a case of political tapping in 1978. During the Grunwick strike, a tap was attached to a telephone used by the strike committee in the Brent Trades Council offices in Willesden Lane. This ran through Harlesden exchange: one local engineer tried to disconnect it, but engineers from the special team rapidly re-installed it. At the same time, Special Branch officers set up surveillance of the Trades Council offices from hired rooms in a nearby pub: long-range microphones were used in an attempt to monitor conversations through windows.

Home and office numbers of union leaders and others involved in major industrial disputes are frequently, even routinely, tapped: M15 appear to take the view that ministers have no 'need to know' about the

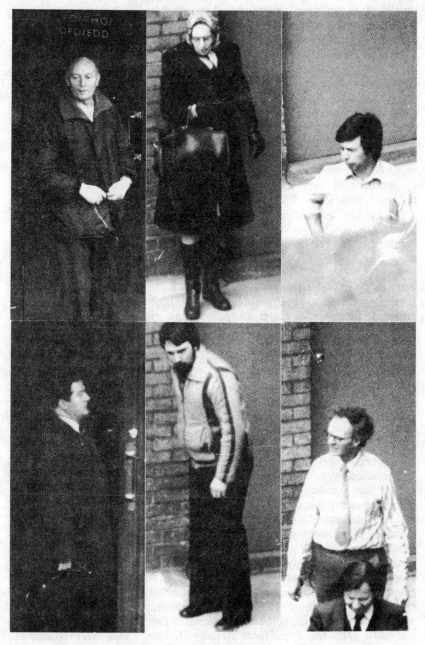

The phone tappers of Ebury Bridge Road

details of surveillance operations. According to the tapping-centre employee who gave us some of the most detailed information, there was no MP's telephone being tapped during the Sixties. Thus, the assurances given by Harold Wilson in 1964 appear to have been honoured.

But it is hard to feel real confidence in any of the informal 'safeguards' which are supposed to exist. Only the police, we were told, stick to the procedure of obtaining a warrant before placing a tap: the secret agencies have a *carte blanche*. Their activities may be covered by a general warrant, which counts only as 'one' in accounts given to ministers, even though hundreds of lines may be involved. (Certainly, GCHQ has a single general warrant allowing all overseas telegrams and cables to be intercepted at will.) Warrants, when they are obtained, are handled by the Police Department of the Home Office; the Home Secretary's signature is obtained with little difficulty and little explanation. Even though ex-Inspector Lee made extensive and highly successful use of phone-taps in Operation Julie, he deplored the risks of abuse in the present arrangements. 'It's an executive decision – there's absolutely no accountability', he said to us.

Threats from technology
If tapping used to be kept within bounds, this probably had more to do with problems of technology and manpower than with any structure of legal control. But the technological changes which upset the balance are only just beginning.

A new generation of British telephone exchanges, known as 'System X', is about to come into service. This, if not regulated, can be turned into a tool of mass-surveillance far more readily than our present cumbersome electro-mechanical exchanges – and there is another shrouded department of the Post Office which appears to be working on just that project.

In today's exchanges, large cables enter from the street, spray out onto distribution frames and are connected to long racks of switching equipment. Everything is highly visible, and comprehensible even to uninstructed eyes.

Every aspect of System X's operation will be concealed inside miniature electronic devices. Its overall operations will be controlled by inaccessible computers, themselves subordinate to regional control centres. Complex facilities for channelling calls through exchanges will anyway be required, and adding a few programmes to monitor 'target' lines will be simple. No dangerously visible extra wires will be required to be attached during semi-clandestine visits: there will be no warning lights, and rather fewer people around each exchange to notice what may be going on.

Analysis of the Post Office Telecommunications HQ Directory – which revealed the 'Equipment Development Division' – points to another odd outfit: OP7, the 'Equipment Strategy Division'. This, later re-labelled as the 'Operational Strategy Co-ordination Division', is a self-contained section of the much larger team working on System X at 6 Lambeth Road

Report of the Committee of Privy Councillors appointed to inquire into the interception of communications

Mr. Merlyn Rees:

......

Legislation is not required to legalise telephone interception. If it is required at all, it would be for the purpose of entrenching in statute the appropriate restrictions and safeguards under which interception is practised. The restrictions and safeguards applicable in this country were scrutinised and commended in 1957 by the Birkett Committee. Its report (Cmnd. 283) has ever since then provided the basis on which interception is carried out, and I can assure the House that it continues to do so today.

I recognise the importance of adequate and effective safeguards for the liberty of the subject................

The Birkett Report was published a quarter-century ago — the first and only public discussion of telephone tapping — yet Home Office ministers persistently reassure Parliament, quite wrongly, that nothing has changed.

SE1. Once again, separate lines of control and meaningless directory entries are pointers to a purpose which cannot be acknowledged.

Several Post Office engineers have told us they believe extensive surveillance capacity is being built into System X. And indeed, little effort can be involved. System X's computers will automatically generate records of who calls whom, when and for how long, as part of their means of operation. Such records, supplied wholesale for secret analysis, could provide means of supervision as exclusive as any state might desire. The first System X exchange – in the City of London – opened in the summer of 1980.

Mail-opening and bugging

The Post Office also opens mail and manufactures bugging equipment. Mail-opening is based on the 290-strong Investigation Division, located in the 25th and 26th floors of the Euston Tower building. The main job of the ID is to detect crimes against the Post Office, but much mail-opening has nothing to do with such aims. Ingenious equipment, including extremely long, thin pliers which enable letters to be rolled-up and removed from envelopes via the corners, are among the devices ID employs. There are also special sprays – one is made by the US firm Du Pont – which turn an envelope temporarily translucent, and special solvents used to ungum flaps.

Still more advanced equipment is already in service, according to two Post Office employees, allowing some mail to be read unopened. This is done by electronic scanning which can detect the carbon used in most kinds of ink. But the underlying mechanics of mail interception remain simple: letters sorted for a particular postman's 'walk' are removed selectively by a postal supervisor or ID Investigation Officer who has a list of 'target' addresses. The mail is then taken by messenger to the main local Post Office, where it is opened by ID officials, read, copied if interesting, and returned to the sorting office.

London's main letter-opening centre is at Union House in St Martin's-le-Grand, close to St Paul's. A 'Special Section' of the Investigation Division is based there: intercepted mail is addressed to the Officer on Duty, Room 202.

The man in charge of this special section is Mr R. F. G. Roberts, aged 58, an Assistant Controller in the Investigation Division. This results from a process of elimination: although Mr Roberts' name appears in official lists of senior Post Office staff, it does not appear in the ID's entry in the Post Office's internal telephone directory. All other ID staff of similar rank appear, and have clearly-described, legitimate functions. Callers who ask for Mr Roberts at the Investigation Division's Euston Tower headquarters are referred to a City number, 432 4209.

When we placed a call to this number we were told that it was indeed the 'Special Section', and that Mr Roberts was in charge, although not present. We said that we were making a press inquiry concerning mail opening: whereupon the official at the other end denied that the Section opened mail, declined to say what business the Section *was* engaged in, and terminated the conversation very abruptly.

The Investigation Division's mail-opening programme has come to light on a number of occasions, the most notable being the case of *Freedom,* the anarchist magazine, in 1972. Intercepted mail which was being returned to the Eastern District Sorting Office in London was delivered to *Freedom* complete with the cover-note from the Special Section to an ID official at the local office. Another well-documented case concerned the Socialist Labour League (now the Worker's Revolutionary Party) in 1967, when one of the messengers involved told them about Post Office mail interception and copying, taking place in a basement adjacent to Union House.

Political groups of many complexions are aware of inteference with their mail, evidenced by the otherwise impossible mixing of mail from wholly-separate postal areas. The Communist Party, for instance, which has its headquarters in King Street, Covent Garden, has often received mail addressed to unlikely locations such as the anarchist bookshop 'Rising

Post Office Research Centre, Martlesham Heath; R12 has top floor offices.

Free', then near Kings Cross Station. Members of the British Society for Social Responsibility in Science have found mail for colleagues living miles away included in their own home deliveries. On some occasions, such as the opening of some of the National Council for Civil Liberties' mail during the Agee-Hosenball case, the work has been done so obviously as to leave little doubt that harassment was intended.

Bugging is part of the work of the R12 'Special Investigations Division' of the Post Office, which is run by Mr M. F. Meads and is located in the extensive new Research Centre at Martlesham Heath near Ipswich. It is well-known in the electronics business that the Division orders considerable quantities of ultra-miniature electronics parts, including microphones. Members of the division have demonstrated bugging devices to security organisations in Britain and overseas.

R12's entry in the official staff directory is as unrevealing as that of its shadowy London counterparts. It contains such meaningless task-descriptions as 'improvements in current practice A' or 'physical investigation B'. Normal job descriptions are highly detailed.

Much of the top floor at Martlesham Heath is devoted to R12. An electronic detector system guards it from entry by other PO researchers (who describe the people involved as 'Faceless'). The only entrance to the section is via a blank room with locked doors, and an intercom on the wall with which to ask for admission. Staff lists show that most of its 117 personnel are technicians, concerned with manufacture and assembly, rather than graduate scientists engaged in research.

Two-and-a-half years ago, R12 engineers secretly visited German security officials to swap information on bugs. At one meeting, they showed off an 'infinity' bug, which could be inserted in a phone and then called up from anywhere else to eavesdrop on conversations.

The official response
We put detailed questions to the Post Office concerning each of the divisions investigated here – specifically inviting them to confirm or deny

that the role of the Chelsea establishment is telephone-tapping. They replied:

> The Post Office has no comment to make. The policy on interception of communications is a matter for the Home Secretary and every case has to be personally approved by a Secretary of State. We refer you to the Home Office.

We then spoke to the Home Office Director of Information, Donald Grant. He said:

> We wouldn't answer questions like that anyway – you know that very well. Successive answers in the House of Commons (make the situation clear). It is not in the public interest that the details be made public. The Birkett report might repay reading . . . it's carried out to the letter.

It is quite clear that the phone-tapping situation has entirely altered since Lord Birkett reported. The document, however, does repay reading in one sense: because even then there was a separate reservation by one of the committee, Mr Patrick Gordon Walker MP, who is and always has been some distance from a wild-eyed radical. He said then:

> . . . I cannot wholly agree with my colleagues that present use of the power to intercept communications should continue unchanged. In my view the purposes for which warrants are issued should in future be judged by stricter standards . . .

Those sensible reservations clearly made no impact upon bureaucratic opinion. Two brief points may be worth making in conclusion. First, the proliferation of phone-tapping equipment may be justified by reference to the 'Irish troubles'. But it seems clear that much of the expansion was planned in the sixties – well before the IRA became a substantial threat. And in any case, much of the extra load thus caused is carried directly by military intelligence facilities.

Second, it may be justified by something resembling a new Cold War hysteria. But that is a reason for stricter, not laxer, legislative supervision. One of the essential discoveries that the Americans made during the seventies was that the burgeoning activities of the 'intelligence community' – wire-tapping, mail-opening and the like – were targeted, in reality, not against the external enemies of the United States, but against the American public itself. That is a painful discovery we are beginning to make in this country. But whether we have the same legal and constitutional means for investigating it is another question.

First published 1 February 1980

CHAPTER THREE

Big Brother's Many Mansions

Cause for concern about the work of the secret intelligence and security services is not confined to their role in telephone tapping and mail opening. The sole accountability of MI5, MI6 and other services to Parliament is through the annual Secret Vote, recently raised to £40m. But this can only be a small part of actual resources allocated. Other funds, we are informed by ex-employees, are 'laundered' away from budgets voted for other purposes: Home, Foreign and Defence.

Between an unquestioned and unquestionable Secret Vote, and the unconstitutional laundering of funds is an enormous void of unaccountability. Many of the security and intelligence agencies' activities — which inevitably, can only be sampled through intense barriers of secrecy and deception — raise deeper problems than secret, unaccountable funds.

Bugging operations are separate from telephone tapping but come under even less legal restraint. Bugging must normally involve some kind of intrusion into premises — even, on occasion, breaking and entering. (but, as in the case of phone-tapping, new technologies are emerging which make the intruder's task even easier, and even harder to control.)

Most of the 'secrets' here are secret only from the British public which pays the bills. There is ample evidence that in several cases Soviet and East European intelligence services have penetrated flimsily-assembled 'covers'.

The government's secret real estate
In London alone, the security and intelligence services appear to have exclusive use of eight large office blocks. This suggests that their official budget – £40 million – must be a serious deception. We have assembled evidence from many public sources, and confirmed with those acquainted with the security agencies and elsewhere, that all the buildings portrayed on the following pages are – or were recently – concerned entirely with such activities. From this – undoubtedly rough – assessment, we can estimate the numbers employed in these premises, and gauge the overall cost.

The legitimate work of these services does of course require office premises of some size. But these London offices appear to employ enough people to consume the entire Secret Vote in salaries alone. We estimate that the salaries of the 5,400 employees in these London offices alone must amount, at the very least, to just under £40 million. Additionally, rates not charged to the Vote amount to £2.3 million, and rental likewise ignored would be over £10 million. Overall, the real budgets for M15, M16 and GCHQ could be more than £300 million. A detailed calculation is included at the end of this report.

The size and power of the spooks may, we suggest, be indicated by the extent of their real estate. In many cases, we know little or nothing about precisely what the building is used for. But in the case of one unit, a great deal has been established from public documents, confirmed by police and intelligence sources.

Bugging centres

A joint electronic surveillance and bugging facility for M15, M16 and the police is located in a quiet part of South London, at 113 Grove Park, Camberwell, SE5. The site is entered by a driveway concealed behind a surburban terrace and overlooking a railway. The only entrance is via an electrically operated steel doorway. Like Tinkerbell, the phone-tapping headquarters, this office is operated 24 hours a day.

Officially, although not publicly, the centre is part of C7 division of the Metropolitan Police, which supplies technical services. Occasionally, public advertisements for recording specialists have referred to the 'Camberwell Tape Laboratory'. The site is marked by a number of high radio masts, many steerable, and capable of receiving a wide range of different radio signals. The role of the centre, a large part of which is said by visitors to be below ground, is confirmed by its entry in the local planning register. It is recorded as a 'wireless receiving station'.

The bugs used by the police and security services are varied in type and facility. Briefly, they enable all conversations in a room or building to be monitored from a distance. The bugs will transmit overhead conversations to a listening centre either by radio or wires – if so, usually telephone wires. The use of a bug is quite distinct from tapping where only conversation held on a telephone can be heard: a bug is at least intended to pick up everything. Planting a bug on a 'target' premises requires, almost by necessity, breaking and entering or, at the very least, gaining entry by deception. As much is admitted by ex-Inspector Dick Lee in his published account of the Operation Julie drug case. If the bug works by radio then its signals on a special Home Office frequency band will be picked up from a nearby office, specially equipped van, or one of a number of fixed listening sites throughout London.

Yet although bugging would appear of necessity to involve officially blessed law-breaking, no warrants are needed to employ bugs on any police investigation. In the Metropolitan Police, bugging is generally authorised by a Deputy Commissioner. But this is no real difficulty, according to one police source, as authority to bug 'can be obtained in five minutes'. The

Left: The distinctively curtained 16th floor of Euston Tower marks the MI5 floor out from those used by the DHSS, above and below. Below: the sturdy barrier which protects the entrance of the bugging HQ concealed in Camberwell, a south London suburb.

Camberwell centre has been involved in important cases where bugging has been necessary and indeed publicly acknowledged – such as the Spaghetti House and Balcombe Street sieges, and other terrorist disturbances. But such cases form only a small part of the centre's work. According to former police and intelligence officials, much of Camberwell's bugging capabilities are used not by the police for criminal investigation, but by the intelligence agencies.

The Metropolitan Police have been closely connected with the intelligence services in the use of electronic espionage for a long time. According to documents now in the Public Records Office, the Camberwell centre – then known as 'Grove Park' – was operated by Metropolitan Police staff in the 1920s and 1930s to intercept radio signals from foreign embassies in London. It supplied information to GCCS, the forerunner of GCHQ (the vast codebreaking and monitoring agency now based at Cheltenham). Later, the bulk of this activity, still in the hands of the police, moved to Sandridge near St Albans. After the war, Sandridge was taken over as a GCHQ listening station. Teams of mobile eavesdropping vans for use throughout Britain were stationed there in the 1950s and early 60s. The police connection continued, and Sandridge has now been taken over by the Home Office as a police and MI5 research centre.

Sandridge continues to develop surveillance and other technical equipment for the Camberwell centre and M15, according to former senior police officers. One of these is the spectacular laser monitoring device which can detect conversations at long range by reflecting a laser beam off a window pane or, better, an object inside a room. M15 placed a security clamp on development of this device by commercial companies in the late 60s, according to one former intelligence agent. On a recent visit to Sandridge, I recognised laser equipment being tested on the centre's roof.

The Post Office is also closely involved in bugging. As mentioned in the previous report, the R12 division at Martlesham Heath near Ipswich manufactures (and has demonstrated) miniature bugs which attach to a telephone or transmit by radio. The R12 division is closely connected with GCHQ and the security services. One estimate of the extent of bugging comes from a Post Office employee, with knowledge of the quantities of miniature printed circuits and other parts ordered by the division. Four hundred were ordered in one year. But the Home Office refuses to give any figures for the number of bugging authorisations made for police or the security services.

Other government departments are involved in the manufacture and use of bugging equipment. The Joint Services Electronics Research Laboratory, near Baldock, has been claimed to be the source of bugs used by military intelligence in Northern Ireland. GCHQ and the Foreign Office jointly run the Diplomatic Telecommunications Maintenance Service, based at Hanslope Park near Milton Keynes and in London. DTMS provides both bugging and debugging specialists who regularly check government offices and embassies for bugs. But they also specialise in installing bugs, and have allegedly done this in No 10 Downing Street during Harold Wilson's administration.

Post Office staff are seconded to DTMS for work in Britain and abroad. According to former intelligence officials, members of DTMS or the Post Office's Chelsea tapping centre may instal bugs by posing as Post Office engineers repairing telephone installations. This allegation was also made by a senior official of a Post Office union who explained how, once bugs were installed on a private phone, official records were doctored to ensure that no ordinary engineer visited the premises and discovered the bug. Each telephone line has a 'Fault Card' maintained on it at the local exchange, he explained, which is consulted before an engineer makes any visit. Once a phone installation is used for bugging, the card will usually be marked 'refer to Special Services'. Special Services is a section in each telephone manager's office which deals with security liaison.

Embassies . . . unions . . . journalists . . .
The major targets of the British bug teams appear to be political. The *Sunday Times* revealed in February 1980 that a massive intelligence attack was mounted in autumn 1979 against Patriotic Front delegates to the Lancaster House conference. Every surveillance resource was employed to try to monitor the conversations and discussions of Nkomo and Mugabe, at all times. Their Special Branch guards – ostensibly provided for protection – were required to find out about their plans for changing hotels, meeting rooms, and pass on details to the intelligence services. The operation was, according to a senior intelligence source, authorised directly by the Prime Minister and Lord Carrington.

Although the intelligence agencies, by means of monitoring all phone calls, diplomatic communications, and bugging meetings, sought to discover each delegation's strategy, they were hardly even-handed. In order to interpret the African languages and dialects used by the PF delegates, Rhodesian security personnel were directly employed in the operation.

It was not the first time that such methods had been used against the Patriotic Front leaders, according to the same sources. Critical meetings during the 1979 non-aligned conference in Havana were bugged by American agents. The information was then passed to Britain through the international link between GCHQ and the National Security Agency, NSA. Mrs Thatcher made a particular point of thanking President Carter for this technical assistance.

A former intelligence official who has worked at one of London's phone-tapping centres has described to us the targets of intelligence bugging and tapping operations:

Embassies, all of them . . . including the Americans . . . trade union leaders and offices all the time . . . journalists, not very many, we've got enough information from inside . . . shipping companies, they're a very valuable source of information . . . a few MPs . . .

Targets of this surveillance have included Labour ministers such as Judith

Hart. Their political aides in the last Labour government have also had their telephones tapped, one intelligence source stated.

M15 in Mayfair

The expensive properties of the intelligence and security services are only part of a much larger scene. Of the three main agencies, M15 (Security Service), M16 (Secret Intelligence Service), and GCHQ (Government Communications HQ), only M15 is concentrated in London. Many M16 personnel are, naturally, based overseas under diplomatic cover. GCHQ's main buildings are in Cheltenham, Gloucestershire, where they occupy considerable premises. Most of GCHQ's personnel and costs are borne on the Defence budget and the cost of operating GCHQ and its UK and overseas monitoring centres is not distinguished in Defence or Foreign Estimates presented to Parliament.

Of the offices pictured in this report, nine are currently in use by one or other of the services (one of them, in Great Marlborough Street, was being refurbished at the time of writing). From ordnance survey maps, the floorspace available in each block may be calculated, leading to our estimate of budget and personnel.

The headquarters of M15 are now at Curzon Street House, Curzon Street, W1. They formerly occupied another block just along the street – Leconfield House, a stone's throw from the Hilton and the Playboy Club. When Leconfield House's owners planned to modernise the block, M15 resolutely refused to move out of Mayfair. Curzon Street House is a solid fortress, built as such during the last war, from which they can adequately resist unwelcome pressures for change.

Several other substantial Mayfair properties swell M15's portfolio. No 71/72 Grosvenor Street, which once housed many of the Security Services' political files, is still in use. Like so many of their offices its cover is blown by contrasting two public directories – a street directory which lists the premises as occupied by MoD (Army), and a civil service directory which fails to mention the place in its MoD (Army) section. A ground floor Estée Lauder cosmetics shop fails to distract attention from obvious government fittings, heavy lace curtains and tight security.

At 41 South Audley Street, W1, a smaller office which lies above a patisserie not far from the US Embassy, M15's cover appears a little better. Unfortunately, they are not helped by the Post Office, who refer enquiries about their telephone number – cunningly listed in a private name, for once – to 'Special Services'. Callers are told: 'That means it's probably a government department'.

The Service's front office, until it moved to the new HQ (apart from their mystifying postal address of 'Box 500') is at 14–17 Great Marlborough Street, opposite trendy Carnaby Street. MI5's legal adviser, who attends trials and meets provincial policeman on their behalf, was based there.

Surveillance of political and 'subversive' activity in the London area is mounted from a number of smaller offices. One such office is the

Above left: MI5's old HQ at Leconfield House, Curzon Street, W1. Above right: MI6 training centre at 296–302 Borough High Street, SE1. Below left: joint MI5 and military intelligence and surveillance offices at 140 Gower Street, WC1. Below right: MI5 Headquarters at Curzon House, Curzon Street, W1.

Above left: GCHQ's London Office, 2/8 Palmer Street, W1. Above right: MI5's front office, 14–17 Great Marlborough Street, W1. Below left: MI5 centre at 71/72 Grosvenor Street, W1. Below right: the MI6 'London Station' at 60 Vauxhall Bridge Road, SW1.

Above: Century House, 100 Westminster Bridge Road, SE1 — the headquarters of the Secret Intelligence Service, MI6. Inset: eavesdropping aerials on the roof, directed at London's embassy land. Right: MI5 undercover office at 41 South Audley Street, Mayfair, W1.

landmark Euston Tower building. The DHSS, who occupy most of the building's first 20 floors (the Post Office have the top half) confirm that the 12th and 16th floors are used by other departments. The 16th floor is noticeably surrounded by heavy curtains, unlike the others. Equally noticeable, until last year, was a mysterious high power scrambled radio signal, probably used to keep in touch with official cars. The signal, from a permanently staffed communications centre at the very top of the building, causes considerable interference in the vicinity, not least to TV and radio studios on the ground floor.

One of M15's more notorious surveillance offices was a large garage at 1-8 Barnard Road, Battersea. Any secrecy attaching to it was fairly thoroughly blown when two East European 'diplomats' were caught trying to break into it in 1968. All the same, M15 did not give up using it for another ten years.

Another office block at 26-28 Mount Row, Mayfair appears to be part of the M15 portfolio. It is listed in local records as central government offices, but the address does not appear in any published civil service directory. A phone book, clearly stamped SECRET, is on display at the building's reception desk. This suggests that the offices are unlikely to belong to any orthodox department of central government (not even the MoD's ordinary internal phone book attracts such high classification).

The Secret Service, M16, has less salubrious facilities. It was banished during the late sixties to Century House, a 20-storey tower block near Waterloo. This is listed publicly as the site of the Foreign Office 'Permanent Under-Secretary's Department', which is the FO's liaison with M16. Its mail is variously sent to 'Box 850' or to a non-existent Mr G. H. Merrick of the Foreign Office. The third floor of an adjacent annexe houses the service's computer centre.

A variety of training centres meet the personnel requirements of M16 and a number of foreign secret services. The principal training department is a stroll away at 296-302 Borough High Street, SE1. More colourful subjects – sabotage, demolition and general mayhem-raising – are taught at an undercover establishment in Gosport called Fort Monkton. This centre, in a Napoleonic fort opposite Portsmouth Harbour, sports a fine selection of security fences, in order to broaden the espionage recruit's experience. All are clearly visible from the adjacent golf course.

One veteran of the Fort Monkton course is the former Norwegian military intelligence agent, Major Sven Blindheim. He told us that he was taught sabotage skills there before being employed by British and US intelligence to train teams of right-wing Finns for operations inside the USSR. (Many of the Finns failed to return, and Blindheim quit the job when he concluded that it was 'illegal'.)

Fort Monkton's secrets are witheld only from the British public. The Russians have been well-informed about the place since 1951, when Kim Philby attended a course there. Officially described as an 'Army Training Establishment', it seems to conform fairly closely to the 'Sarratt' training centre in John Le Carré's novels. TV cameras guard the entrance, and track the movements of inquisitive visitors.

Sir Francis Brooks Richards, a Deputy Secretary in the Cabinet Office. His role of Co-ordinator of Security and Intelligence removes the accountability of the security services from government ministers.

Brooks Richards is now co-ordinator of Security in Northern Ireland. His place has been taken by Sir Anthony Duff.

Men at the Top

Another unacknowledged department, the Cabinet Office Joint Intelligence Staffs provides overall direction for all three secret services. The person in charge (under the Secretary to the Cabinet) is Sir Francis Brooks Richards, Co-ordinator of Intelligence and Security. His position is a powerful one: he needs to answer only to a few committees of officials, and to the Prime Minister. Inquiries into the Cabinet Committee structure by the *New Statesman* in 1978 did not reveal (under Labour) any ministerial committee for the oversight of intelligence and security, although regular reports were –

and presumably are – made to the committee handling defence and foreign affairs. Brooks Richard's immediate predecessor was Sir Leonard Hooper, a former director of GCHQ.

The possibility that the intelligence and security services might drift into political 'dirty tricks' was not lessened by Mrs Thatcher's appointment of an extremely right-wing minister to liaise with the Co-ordinator. Angus Maude, the Paymaster-General, was given this role, together with an overt responsibility for government 'information policy' – bluntly, propaganda. The role has some similarities with that given to George Wigg by Harold Wilson in the sixties. (Maude's job was to have gone to the late Airey Neave.)

M15 is now run by Sir Howard Trayton Smith, a former ambassador to Moscow and one-time 'British government representative in Northern Ireland'. Since the British Government does not need diplomatic representation in Northern Ireland, this may be read as a euphemism for the security co-ordination job now publicly assigned to Sir Maurice Oldfield, former director of M16.

Sir Arthur ('Dickie') Franks, reputedly a hard-liner with Thatcherite ideas, now runs M16. Formerly he was deputy to Oldfield, who was regarded by the standards of the intelligence world as something of a liberal. Brian Tovey, tall and bespectacled and formerly in charge of the Communications Electronic Security Group, heads GCHQ.

What hope is there that sovereignty over all these lush but shadowy empires might be returned to Parliament? In the short term, not much. Curiously, the fact that almost every penny of Secret Service expenditure was until recently illegal has come to light only as part of the attempt to reassert Parliamentary authority. Robin Cook MP has unearthed the formidable Civil List and Secret Service Act of 1782, which prohibited the government from spending more than £10,000 a year on secret services. This Act was only repealed in 1977, after nearly two centuries of illegal overspending.

Parliamentary questions have also established that the Ministry of Defence started 'laundering' funds for security and intelligence activities in 1946.

Just now, MI5 is authorised to withhold any details of its activities from ministers, as well as from Parliament, unless it considers they have a 'need to know'. That, of course, is a charter for writing your own cheques, taking over any premises you fancy, phone-tapping, bugging and generally snooping on any sections of the population who don't share the Cabinet Office view of life.

The Labour Party's Home Affairs Study Group on the intelligence services finally got under way after Tony Benn's much-publicised initiative in 1979. Previously Labour had never tackled the issue really seriously, and certainly did not take advantage of its periods of office to submit the secret agencies to any democratic oversight. But the realisation may be spreading that the new technologies of surveillance make the challenge genuinely

Above: the Sarratt 'Nursery' of John Le Carre's fictional Secret Service appears to correspond to this real life sabotage, demolition and agent training centre: Fort Monkton, at Gosport, Hampshire. Below: a variety of British and foreign government secutiry fences are part of the trainees' hurdles.

urgent; that unless they are legally defended, our traditional liberties will not long survive.

Footnote: Measuring up the spooks

Using 1:1250 Ordnance Survey plans, we calculated the floor space of all the known London offices in use. The grand total is just over 100,000 square metres. The Property Services Agency, which provides and maintains all government offices, say that as a first estimate they allocate 200 square feet (18.4m^2) of gross office space per head in London accommodation. The buildings discussed here will therefore accommodate about 5,400 people.

The *Supply Estimates 1979-80* gives the overall salary costs, including superannuation, of each central government department. The security and intelligence services probably offer similar remuneration to the Foreign Office (average cost £9,984 yearly), or the Cabinet Office (£7,350). Even on the lower figure, staff costs alone would not leave much change out of the £40 million 'Secret Vote'.

The cost of providing the buildings, met directly by the Property Services Agency, would begin with about £2.3 million in rates. Rents at normal commercial levels would be at least £10 million (some nice real estate is involved).

Operating costs, of course, only begin with salaries. In the case of the Foreign Office, total costs are about 2.5 times salary cost. For other departments, the ratio is much smaller, but spies hardly come cheaper than diplomats. So long as we have to guesstimate, it seems reasonable to put the costs of M15 and M16 together as being rather more than £100 million a year.

First published 8 February 1980

CHAPTER FOUR

The Facts Behind the Official Line

The eight-page White Paper on the 'Interception of Communications in Great Britain'*, published in April 1980, looked slim indeed, when compared to the detailed 40-page report on the same subject which Lord Birkett and others submitted almost 23 years ago. Both reports omit a good many salient facts; the 1980 version is the most serious offender.

Its chief deception is that it makes no mention of the principal government department working on the interception of communications in Britain: Government Communications Headquarters (GCHQ). Thousands of people are directly or indirectly employed in its signals 'intelligence' (SIGINT) activities in Britain. Nor are they solely concerned with, for example, breaking the secret codes of foreign powers. The tapping centre in Chelsea known to the police as 'Tinkerbell' was designed, and much of its equipment provided by GCHQ. GCHQ also receives much of Tinkerbell's intelligence, as do the other, better known agencies, M15 and M16.

The White Paper did not deny our report; it merely avoided the issue by noting that the warrants discussed therein are issued for the

purposes (of) the police, HM Customs and Excise and the Security Service (M15) . . .

Neither GCHQ nor the Secret Intelligence Service (M16) are included in the list; yet all are substantial users of information from intercepted communications.

The 'safeguards' in the tapping rules were published with the White Paper; but they fall a long way short of balancing personal and political liberty with the need to serve the public interest. In the case of tapping by the police, the restrictions sound fine:

the offence must be really serious; normal methods of investigation

*Command 7873, published by HMSO.

> must . . . from the nature of things be unlikely to succeed . . . interception would be likely to lead to arrest and conviction.

But 'serious' doesn't mean what it used to mean. It normally means an offence with a likely minimum sentence of three years' imprisonment, but it can also mean

> an offence of lesser gravity in which either a large number of people is involved or there is a good reason to apprehend the use of violence . . .

This could be interpreted to cover any industrial dispute or 'political' case.

The 'safeguards' affecting the Security Service are significantly weaker, since no offence need ever take place; the SS merely have to demonstrate that interception will 'be of direct use in compiling the information that is necessary . . . in carrying out (its) tasks'. The target of the interception must be 'major subversive, terrorist or espionage activity' – but the current Home Office definition of what constitutes subversion is so wide as to permit the inclusion of much ordinary trades union and even Labour Party activity.

The report admits that warrants for a 'target' organisation, person or activity exist and may cover multiple lines without restriction on the total involved. Thus, the number of warrants issued is less than the number of lines they cover – substantially less, according to our sources. The existence of 'general' warrants, which specify a general target only, and allow civil servants to add or remove the telephone lines involved at will, was admitted, if somewhat elliptically. The White Paper explains that the Secretary of State 'may delegate' to the civil service power to amend a warrant. In other words, once the Home Secretary has approved a single warrant to tap the telephone line of a 'target' organisation, 50 more lines of individual members could be added without his consent being needed.

There are further discrepancies between the number of warrants issued and the number of lines tapped. Clement Freud MP spotted one, and asked Mr Whitelaw

> whether the number of interception orders is cumulative – that is to say, those currently in force – or is the number given simply that of the new orders that have been published?

Whitelaw didn't answer the question, leaving open the possibility that 'permanent' warrants for M15 and the Special Branch (which are re-authorised every six months) are only enumerated once – in the year in which they were first issued. The cumulative number of warrants in force would thus be rather more than that implied by the yearly total published in the White Paper.

Freud also unsuccessfully asked Whitelaw to reveal the breakdown of the totals between Customs and Excise, MI5, and police. But the Home Office, inadvertently, has given a clue to the answer. The White Paper, in a separate table, included figures for the number of warrants signed and in operation at the end of three sample years. These figures may be compared with the total number of warrants signed during the year:

Year	Signed during year	In force at 31 Dec.
1958	129	95
1968	333	155
1978	428	214

Since a normal warrant lasts only two months, the number of warrants said to be in operation at the year's end is astonishingly high. Since warrants for taps by the Special Branch and MI5 are normally renewed for six months at a time, the likely explanation is that most of the warrants go to those agencies, and that many warrants are more or less permanent. On the basis of simple assumptions and some simple maths (warrants issued evenly through the year, and say, once) the proportion of 'security' warrants may be calculated. For 1968 and 1978, the proportion is about 75 per cent.

The numerous opportunities for fiddling the figures, detailed above, go a considerable distance towards explaining the discrepancy between the apparently 'modest' overall figures for warrants issued, and the capacity (of more than 1,000 lines) of the national phone tapping centre in Ebury Bridge Road, London, SW1, where the warrants are put into action by the Post Office. Merlyn Rees told journalists in February 1980 that during his time as Home Secretary, 2-3,000 lines were tapped every year, and 250-400 warrants were in force at any one time. Two months later, Rees greeted the White Paper's rather smaller figures with an almost audible sigh, and a sycophantic speech. He did not offer any suggestions as to how his memory had previously failed him – or, more likely in which way the Home Office had obligingly doctored the real figures down to more 'modest' levels.

At least Whitelaw did acknowledge that some tapping, particularly in Northern Ireland, was not covered by the White Paper. The House of Commons was told that tapping in Northern Ireland was done under the same 'conditions and safeguards';

subject only to overriding requirements for dealing with terrorism . . . which means, in effect, no safeguards for liberty or privacy at all.

There was no mention of the warrants for tapping which are signed by the Foreign Secretary (for GCHQ and SIS), or by the Prime Minister; nor was there any mention of the (reputedly) delegated power of the Cabinet Secretary to sign warrants on the PM's behalf. This whole area was omitted even from the Birkett report. It became clear in 1967 that a permanent warrant authorising the interception of overseas telegrams by GCHQ was in force when Birkett reported – but the subject wasn't touched.

This omission is even more important in the 1980s. The continuing reequipment of the telephone tapping operation changed it from a highly specific and comparatively easily regulated activity, closely linked to clear offences and areas of concern, to generalised intelligence – gathering and surveillance, carried out as part of GCHQ's recognised COMINT job – but turned inward on the British people. The sudden drop in Home Secretary's warrants after 1975 may be one indication that the surveillance 'load' on

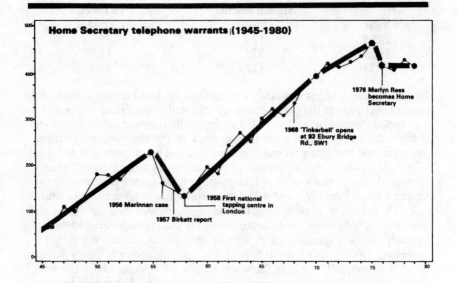

Home Secretary telephone warrants (1945-1980)

1976 Merlyn Rees becomes Home Secretary

1968 'Tinkerbell' opens at 93 Ebury Bridge Rd., SW1

1956 Marinnan case

1957 Birkett report

1958 First national tapping centre in London

HOW MANY WARRANTS ARE ISSUED?

The White Paper 'brings up to date' the Birkett report on the interception of communications, and gives statistics from 1958 to 1979 on warrants issued by the Home Secretary and the Secretary of State for Scotland. The figures, on careful examination, do not bear out Mr Whitelaw's contention that there has been a 'modest overall increase' in the total amount of interception – even leaving aside the omissions and other aspects of the White Paper.

By plotting the newly released figures, a very different picture emerges (see graphs). Warrants for tapping in Scotland, according to the published information were virtually non-existent until 1967. During 1967-69, the number of warrants issued annually was ten or less. During 1979, 56 warrants were issued in Scotland.

The rise in the number of Home Secretary's telephone tapping warrants issued yearly in England and Wales is less startling. From an immediate postwar low of 56, the number of warrants issued rose to peak at 231 in 1955. Thereafter, it has slumped, probably for two reasons. First cold war security hysteria was coming to an end. Second, public concern about telephone tapping was at a peak in 1956/7, provoked by a 1956 case in which telephone tapping information had been passed outside the public service, and which led to the setting up of the Birkett Inquiry in June 1957.

After Birkett there came a sharp boom – from 129 warrants in 1958 to 468 in 1975 – a rise of more than 250 per cent. As can be seen clearly from the trend of the graph, the rise began immediately after Birkett reported, and recommended that in future figures on tapping should not be made public. The rise continued through the 60s, long before international terrorism, invoked by Whitelaw

*Command 7873, published by HMSO.

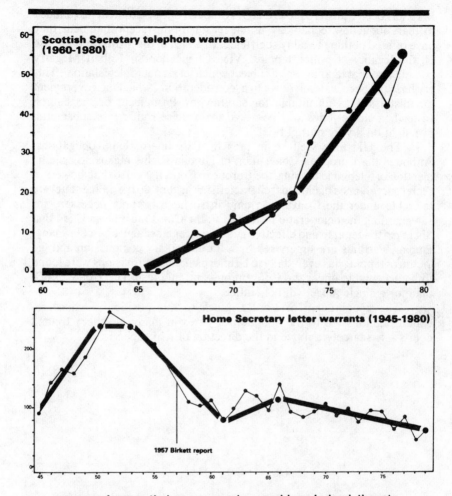

Scottish Secretary telephone warrants (1960-1980)

Home Secretary letter warrants (1945-1980)

1957 Birkett report

as a case for growth, became a serious problem. Indeed, the rate of growth of tapping seems, if anything, to have slackened around 1970, just when terrorist activities were beginning to make their mark.

The most startling feature of the graph is the abrupt dip and levelling off which takes place in 1976. The reason for this feature is unclear from evidence published so far. It clearly does not relate to tight security reins which Merlyn Rees might claim to have imposed after his arrival at the Home Office from Northern Ireland.

The only downward trend is in the number of warrants issued for mail interception. Part of the explanation may be in the removal or downgrading of offences concerning the transmission of, for example, obscene material through the post.

M15 has been transfered to GCHQ. Although the government has alluded to 'fears about new technology' as one reason for the recent statement, they have offered nothing to allay such fears. In 1979, in the *Malone* court case on the legality of police tapping, Vice Chancellor Sir Robert Megarry commented that tapping was a subject which 'cries out for legislation'. This cry has now been watered down to a 'consideration', which the government has dismissed as unsuitable for scrutiny by Parliament or the courts. Instead, a single judge will be asked to exercise rather less substantial oversight on a very partial brief.

The UK may well be in breach of its international obligations. Although the European Convention of Human Rights makes no specific mention of telephone tapping, the European Court has ruled that 'powers of secret surveillance of citizens, characterising as they do the police state, are tolerable under the Convention only in so far as strictly necessary for safeguarding the democratic institutions'; the Court must be satisfied that 'there exist adequate and effective guarantees against abuse'. In Germany, tapping warrants are supervised by a Parliamentary commission and the victim of tapping has eventually to be informed: these provisions were found to be acceptable under the Convention –but only just. The Home Office plan for a single judge will not suffice.

The appointment of Lord Diplock to this position – whose re-commendations led to the abolition of juries in many Northern Ireland courts – is scarcely a move in the direction of real supervision.

CHAPTER FIVE

America's Big Ear in Europe

'Tinkerbell' is only one part of a massive exercise in spying on civil and commercial communications. A much bigger role is played by America's highly secretive National Security Agency (NSA), operating from a remarkable base at Menwith Hill, eight miles west of Harrogate in Yorkshire.

Menwith Hill — unless the KGB has something even bigger — appears to be the biggest tapping centre in the world. From its heavily guarded operations room special high-capacity cables run underground to the Post microwave tower at Hunters Stones five miles away: this provides an umbilical link into the international telephone and telex system running through Britain. A direct tap which is placed on lines to France and elsewhere in Europe has been in operation for more than 15 years.

Five years ago Congressional inquiries uncovered some traces of the NSA's wholesale interception of American and other civilian communications. But the agency has stubbornly resisted all subsequent attempts to discuss any details of its $10–12 billion-worth of operations — so much so as to arouse judicial susicions that they are unconstitutional. Menwith Hill, with rather more than 800 employees working around the clock to gather political, military and economic intelligence, is the largest NSA civilian listening-post — reflecting Britain's strategic position in the world communications net — but even trivial details have been kept secret from the US Congress.

The base at Menwith Hill covers 562 closely-guarded acres of the Yorkshire Moors, festooned with a remarkable array of satellite-tracking aerials. Its business for more than fifteen years has been sifting the communications of private citizens, corporations and governments for information of political or economic value to the US intelligence community: and since the early 1960s its close partner in an operation of ever-growing technical sophistication has been the British Post Office.

The Post Office has built Menwith Hill into the heart of Britain's national communications system – and Britain, of course, occupies a nodal position in the communications of the world, especially those of Western Europe. It is not an exaggeration to say that the first stage of the Post Office's microwave network was constructed around Menwith Hill and its operations: at least five high-capacity networks feed into the base, from all parts of Britain, through the nearby Post Office tower at Hunters Stones (see map, and illustration).

One tap which we can anatomise in considerable detail – due to the documentary indiscretion of a Ministry of Works surveyor – connects at least 3,600 London-to-Paris phone lines to the listeners at Menwith Hill.

The Ministry of Defence told us that the station 'exists with the full approval of the British government'. They did not deny that it intercepted international civil communications on a massive scale but a spokesman claimed that it did not listen in on calls across the Atlantic to or from Britain, 'or any domestic calls in the UK'.

This cautious and partial denial – the Post Office, as always, declines to discuss questions of interception – fails to deal with most of the points we have put to the Ministry. No attempt is made to deny the interception of phone calls to and from Europe, including those from North America: nor is the interception of non-telephone communication, such as telex and telegram traffic, denied. Since most of the operations of the 'big ear' at Menwith Hill would presumably be concentrated on the European side of Britain's communications, the MoD does not appear to be denying any pertinent part of our description. Given the almost total unreliability of official statements about communications interception, it is hard to know how seriously to take any part of the MoD's attempts to explain away the remarkable facilities at Menwith Hill. We have acquired some evidence suggesting that one of the base's minor roles involves the interception of phone-calls between Ireland and the UK: some gesture towards assistance with the anti-IRA campaign might make the existence of Menwith Hill more palatable to the host government. The MoD has refused to comment on suggestions that Menwith Hill could run taps on individual phone lines in Britain – such as those of people campaigning against cruise missile deployment. And a recent statement by a former US Air Force colonel who supervised some National Security Agency operations during the sixties reinforces the point that everything going across the Atlantic can be read by the NSA somewhere. Colonel Fletcher Prouty stated in October 1979 that:

> there are three satellites over the Atlantic, each capable of transmitting on about 20,000 circuits. There are eight transatlantic cables with about 5,000 circuits. NSA monitors all these circuits, collects and records the electronic information transmitted, and its computers can pick out the messages it wants by 'key words'.

Every aspect of Menwith Hill's operations is shrouded in secrecy. But we have been informed that it was specially identified, during secret sessions of the 1975 Congressional hearings on US intelligence agencies, and described as the larger of two centres for tapping telephone lines in Europe.

Three past and present US intelligence officials also confirmed the role of the base from first hand knowledge.

One ex-NSA analyst told us that he had seen a document giving the 'secret all-civilian base' authority for 'tapping the telephone lines to Europe'. A high ranking intelligence consultant, who still works for the US intelligence community, told us that he was aware of Menwith Hill's elaborate telephone and telex tapping facilities. He had inspected the station over 15 years ago, and agreed that it was still engaged in tapping; 'I know it for sure', he said.

One former British military officer has had occasion to visit Menwith Hill's computer vaults. He discovered that 'it intercepts telephone and other communications to and from the United States and Europe. Computers file intelligence dossiers on European political and trades union leaders.'

Self-contained and ultra-secret

The base was first planned in 1954, but did not start operations until 1960. Initially, it was run by the US Army Security Agency, the military monitoring arm of the NSA. In September 1960, a US Army general inaugurated Menwith Hill as the 13th US Army Security Agency Field Station.

The Post Office scheme of secret links also began in 1954, and the planning and construction of both the base and its tapping network proceeded side by side until the early 1960s. The tapping network was concealed within a Post Office plan for a chain of microwave radio towers like the one in central London; this system, named 'Backbone', was supposedly going to provide emergency links if Britain were attacked. But when, after some delay, Backbone was completed, it turned out to be feeding signals into the intelligence base at Menwith Hill instead.

In August 1966, both the 13th ASA Field Station and a subsidiary base at Kirknewton near Edinburgh abruptly closed. Civilians from the National Security Agency took Menwith Hill over entirely, and it became, as it has remained, self-contained and ultra-secret.

The legality of the NSA's operations in Yorkshire may be open to doubt. Under section 4 of the Official Secrets Act of 1920, any Secretary of State can issue a warrant for the interception of telegrams and telephone calls in and out of Britain. But the Post Office Act of 1969, which was used to justify domestic telephone tapping in 1979, only allows Post Office employees to intercept telephone calls for 'crown servants'. Americans are not crown servants.

The Post Office has refused to comment, and says that interception 'is dealt with by the Home Office'. Peter Archer MP, who as Solicitor General in 1979 defended the government's orthodox tapping in criminal cases, told the *New Statesman* that such a massive snooping exercise 'was clearly not intended by Parliament in passing the two Acts.'

Last week the MoD were 'not prepared to answer' when asked how many people worked at Menwith Hill. But a 1974 release dealing with the installation of one of its conspicuous tracking dishes said it had a staff of 800, and since then its facilities have certainly expanded considerably. All employees have to work under rigid security control. Family members are ordered never to mention 'NSA', and all, including children aged twelve and over, are instructed to report all contacts with 'foreign nationals'. Officials and their families have been quickly sent home for even minor indiscretions of teenage children.

NSA surveillance of international telephone lines was admitted officially when CIA Director William Colby appeared before the Pike Committee on Intelligence in 1975. But no details were revealed.

Since Colby's statement, NSA has faced repeated action in the Supreme Court by individuals and groups whose ordinary and legal civil communications were intercepted. NSA has repeatedly refused to disclose details of how it came to intercept their phone calls or telegrams, pleading that disclosure would damage 'vital SIGINT (signals intelligence) sources'.

Heading the list of facilities which NSA does not wish discussed in public is Menwith Hill. So far, no court has forced NSA to the point of disclosure, but some have decided that NSA's reluctance implies that they have illegally breached the US Constitution.

Centre of Britain's radio links
Five miles south of Menwith Hill, a freshly painted sign marked 'Post Office Engineering Department – Private' denies access to a small patch of hilltop woodland. Within the woods is the Hunters Stones Post Office

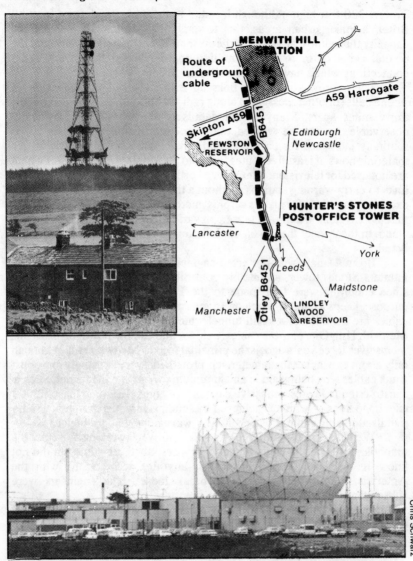

The map labels:

MENWITH HILL STATION
Route of underground cable
Skipton A59
A59 Harrogate
B6451
FEWSTON RESERVOIR
↑Edinburgh Newcastle
HUNTER'S STONES POST OFFICE TOWER
Lancaster
York
Otley B6451
Leeds
Maidstone
Manchester
LINDLEY WOOD RESERVOIR

Chris Schwarz

Menwith Hill Station (above) is the largest and most secret civilian overseas base of the giant US National Security Agency. Its 'dragnet' monitoring of international telephone and telex lines depends on a special network of microwave radio connections, which converge on the tower at Hunters Stones (top left), west of Harrogate, Yorks. From here, a high capacity underground cable (map, top right) runs along the B6451 road, and crosses the Skipton-Harrogate road into the base.

Tower, 320 feet high. Although isolated in the moors and away from all Britain's major urban areas, this tower has a greater communications capacity than almost all others in the system. Hunters Stones is virtually the pivotal point of more than a million route-miles of microwave radio connections which have been installed in Britain.

The microwave network links up Britain by sending thousands of phone calls (or other messages) along radio beams between towers roughly thirty miles apart. Many of the details of the system are physically observable, or can be worked out from information which has to be routinely published for engineers and others: exhaustive analysis of this material shows at least five routes feed into the Hunters Stones tower which are not used for television, telex or even orthodox defence purposes such as links to early-warning stations. Although there are conceivably even more exotic explanations for all this surplus microwave power, the obvious one is that the 'mystery' beams are taps upon various aspects of the whole system – and, in the case of the tap on the London-Paris beam, it can be traced in detail.

From a small, well-protected engineering building at the base of the Hunters Stones tower, a remotely controlled television camera, installed since enquiries were first made to the Post Office about the station's purpose, keeps a careful watch on anyone approaching. Below ground, five cables are installed in a small tunnel which runs beside the road north to Menwith Hill. One of these cables, paid for and installed by the Americans themselves three years ago, is the principal feed to Menwith Hill. Although only about two inches in diameter, it is protected – very unusually for robust trunk cables – by being laid in an aluminium tray within the tunnel. Such a construction indicates a massive capacity — equivalent to at least 32,000 telephone lines — which is achieved by sending very high frequency radio signals along the cable. It is probably a 'waveguide' of very high capacity.

We visited Post Office engineers who were working to replace a manhole cover on the cable tunnel. They described the cable but did not know its purpose. They said that if anything went wrong with the Americans' cable 'all hell would break loose'. The engineers were subsequently warned not to speak to reporters.

During March 1980, a *Sunday Times* photographer took a picture of the secret US cable in its protective tray. However, after that a literal cover-up took place. When a *New Statesman* photographer visited the area four months later, new covers had been installed over the cable and padlocked down, concealing it from view. The new covers are in addition to the normal manhole covers, which are 8 inches thick and weigh several hundredweight. The sign and surveillance camera at Hunters Stones were also new.

The then Menwith Hill Station Commander, Albert D Braeuninger, does not deny the existence of the link to the Post Office. In an interview, he explained:

> We pass information through the UK communications system. Our line is cable . . . it is purely a communications link. We only use the

Hunters Stones power as a customer of the Post Office.
Another NSA official has acknowledged that the main cable to Hunters
Stones was indeed 'high capacity'. The Post Office have refused to answer
any questions, and will only say that 'Hunters Stones is one of our
microwave relay stations. The details of routing of circuits over the
microwave network is something we don't discuss publicly'.

'No high-ranking Brits'

Menwith Hill is completely and carefully isolated from the local community. Many of its staff live on an estate within the base security fence, or
on other specially built housing estates. All their supplies come from a duty
free 'PX' shop, and the base has its own water supply generators, sewage
facilities, fire station, petrol station, restaurants and entertainment facilities.
The outer perimeter is guarded by Ministry of Defence police, who have no
idea as to the purpose of the base. They maintain regular patrols, which
question anyone stopping in the vicinity. The heart of the base is two
massive concrete operations blocks, both extending several floors below
ground, housing hundreds of millions of dollars worth of computer,
communications, and satellite tracking equipment. The 'ops' area is
surrounded by a triple wire fence and has armed guards.

Even outside the operations area, many offices can only be entered by
means of combination lock codes. Although base commander Braeuninger
claimed that the base was a joint facility, the spouse of a former senior
Menwith Hill official gave a different account:

There were no high ranking Brits. They did all the menial jobs like
cleaning, maintenance and electricians for the houses.

The security precautions were intense:

Anyone over 12 going abroad is briefed first. I was taken to Fort
Meade (NSA headquarters near Washington) and had a session with
a security officer on my own. (No-one else) was allowed to be present.
I was told that if I made friends with 'foreign nationals' – that included
Brits – I was to tell my security officer assigned to me . . . We were
never to mention NSA.

Such secrecy extends to US Congressional Committees, to whom
Menwith Hill is a 'classified location' whose operations cannot be divulged.
During a March 1976 appropriations hearing, NSA's Assistant Director
for Installations and Logistics, Brigadier General Charles Knudson, asked
for appropriations to lease 274 family houses for 'a classified location
overseas'. In fact, NSA only has one overseas civilian installation of any
size – Menwith Hill. More housing was required 'due to relocation of
overseas missions and assumption of a new mission'. The secret station's
work, he said, required 47 dwellings at various locations and, revealingly,
'two . . . leases (for) our senior representatives at London, England'.

Aerials for 'Sigint Birds'

The most striking feature of Menwith Hill, to the casual visitor, is the array of satellite communications aerials, tracking dishes and protective 'radomes', which amply fill its skyline. Menwith Hill's space communications facilities have boomed since the first two dishes were installed in 1974. There are now eight, forming part of NSA's worldwide network linking Fort Meade with bases in Germany and Diego Garcia in the Indian Ocean – and making Menwith Hill perhaps the largest known satellite communications terminal in the world.

The purpose of this massive capacity is not entirely apparent. According to one US government communications official, it includes ground stations for top secret CIA and NSA satellites designed to monitor civil communications from countries whose telecommunications administrations are less obliging then the British Post Office. These satellites, colloquially known as 'Sigint birds', include CIA projects RHYOLITE and ARGUS, whose existence was only revealed recently during a spy trial in Los Angeles. (Rhyolite is a dull volcanic rock containing colourful bits of quartz and feldspar – an apt label for a programme which is concerned with hosing up via satellite masses of communications and using computer power to select items of interest.)

CIA officials, as well as those of NSA, work at Menwith Hill. One of them, Larry Schott (now returned to the US), was indiscreet enough to produce his identity card – clearly marked 'Central Intelligence Agency' – to a respected Harrogate journalist a few years ago during a particularly lively party.

Despite such slips, the worst that Harrogate has ever heard about Menwith Hill was a rumour in the early 1970s that the operations blocks were a centre for breeding 'killer flies'. This rumour was, very reasonably, denied.

Who are the targets?
The world had little idea of the scale of this operation until 6 August 1975, when CIA Director William Colby faced determined questioning from Democrat Les Aspin, on the Pike Congressional Committee, about NSA monitoring of 'telephone calls between American citizens and foreigners abroad'. Colby replied that:

> The Agency does monitor foreign communications . . . that go abroad or are abroad. (Traffic with a US citizen at one end) cannot be separated from the traffic that is being monitored.

Neither he nor NSA Director General Lew Allen would go further in open session.

We have, however, obtained copies of both the secret Pike report (which was later leaked to the *Village Voice* newspaper) and further details of the secret testimony on the monitoring of all foreign communications traffic. In 1976, the Pike Committee reported that:

> NSA systematically intercepts international communications, both voice and cable. Messages to and from American citizens have been picked up in the course of gathering foreign intelligence.

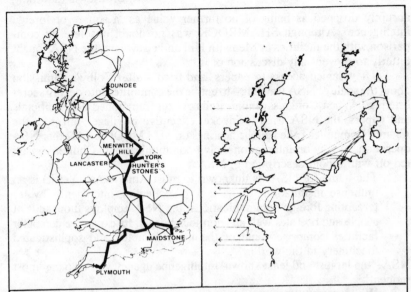

Britain is the hub of international communications to, from and within Europe. The international network (right) is composed of submarine cables and satellite ground stations. Britain's position means that London handles most transatlantic traffic, as well as calls to and from Scandinavia, and northern and eastern Europe. In the early 1960s the special network of Post Office towers and links was built to feed national and international connections into Menwith Hill (left: special links, bold).

During the secret hearing of the Pike Committee, NSA Director Allen gave a more detailed account of how this occurred. According to one firsthand source, Allen did identify two principal British sites for this project – one in the Harrogate area and the other in 'southern England'.

But the operation which could be partially-glimpsed in post-Watergate inquiries into the intelligence agencies' operations had been quietly growing ever since 1945 – it represents, as in Britain, a determination by secret bureaucracies to hold on to powers acquired during the Second World War, and expand them into new technological environments. Four days after VJ day, the Army Security Agency told the American commercial communications corporations that they must continue to hand over copies of all overseas telegrams.

The companies were uneasy, for to do so in peacetime was illegal, but the procedure became institutionalised under the title SHAMROCK, being taken over by the NSA when it succeeded to the Army Security Agency's operations in the fifties.

By spring 1975 the Senate Intelligence Committee under Senator Frank Church finally got wind of SHAMROCK, and in May it was abruptly dropped as being of no further value as 'a source of foreign intelligence'. Although SHAMROCK was no doubt obsolete by comparison with the facilities at Menwith Hill and elsewhere, the NSA fought bitterly to prevent any discussion of it.

They denied access to papers, and tried – after Colby's admission about the scale of NSA trawling – to entice the committee into deeply secret briefings. When Congresswoman Bella Abzug summoned NSA officials and papers, the NSA tried to invoke 'executive privilege'; angered, the Church Committee called public hearings on SHAMROCK and other NSA operations spying on international civil communications. Church himself led off with a bold description of NSA:

> The name (of NSA) is unknown to most Americans. (Yet it) is an immense installation. In its task of collecting intelligence by intercepting foreign communications, the NSA employs thousands of people and operates with an enormous budget. Its expansive computer facilities comprise some of the most complex and sophisticated machinery in the world.

NSA, 'the largest and least known' intelligence agency was also the 'most reticent':

> While it sweeps in messages from around the world, it gives out precious little information about itself . . . no statute establishes the NSA or defines the permissible scope of its activities.

Church concluded triumphantly:

> We will bring the agency from behind closed doors.

NSA 'watch lists'

The Church Committee didn't quite do that. While they exposed SHAMROCK and other illegal NSA operations, they gave no public indication whether similar activities were continuing. In fact, SHAMROCK had started becoming obsolete in 1962, when NSA 'was able to sort electronically the information wanted . . . against its selection criteria.'

Few specific details of these electronic searches are known. We have however pieced together details of HARVEST, a massive NSA computer purpose-built by IBM, which was delivered to NSA headquarters in 1962.

HARVEST was the biggest computer built until the late 60s. At its centre was an IBM processor known as STRETCH, coupled to HARVEST units which were capable of sifting intercepted communications at phenomenal speed. HARVEST could look for words of intelligence significance while working at a rate of 4 million characters a second – roughly equivalent to reading, sorting and filing everything in a large daily newspaper in less than a second. (It was also specially designed for codebreaking).

Menwith Hill, we have learnt, received a similar but smaller IBM computer at about the same time, based on an IBM 7094 processor.

These computers, and manual analysts elsewhere, used then and still use a procedure called 'watch lists' for sorting information. The watch lists contain names of political figures, businesses, and other topics of interest.

The extent of NSA surveillance of targets unrelated to 'national security' is breathtaking. From published articles, and private information from more than half a dozen former NSA employees, we have compiled an extensive list of organisations or individuals whose calls and telegrams were intercepted, or who were on 'watch lists'. They include:

> Former US Attorneys-General Ramsay Clark and Robert F Kennedy; Texas Governor John Connally; civil rights and black activists Jane Fonda, Dr Benjamin Spock, Tom Hayden, Rev Ralph Abernathy (who succeeded Martin Luther King), Eldridge Cleaver, Abbie Hoffman, Stokely Carmichael; foreign leaders Holden Roberto and Robert Mugabe; Detroit attorney Abdeen Jabara, who defended Robert Kennedy's alleged killer; Occidental Oil Corporation; the Scientology organisation; and so on.

Messages referring to these and others, including 75,000 US citizens, had been compiled by NSA computers and analysts up to 1974. Naturally, the US names featuring in NSA files are a small proportion of the Agency's output. The Church Committee noted that 'the great majority of names on the watch list have always been foreign citizens and organisations.' Their composition would be similar to that of the US list:

> members of radical political groups, from celebrities to ordinary citizens involved in protests against their government.

During 1974, the NSA collection of hundreds of thousands of files on foreign citizens and organisations was transferred to a new computer databank, called COINS (Community Online Intelligence System), which is used by NSA, CIA and the Defence Intelligence Agency, DIA. NSA is, according to one COINS analyst, by far the largest user. COINS is now used to file much of the information originating from bases like Menwith Hill. Its scope is broad, according to one report. By 1974, its spread of US citizens under surveillance included:

> prominent Americans in business, the performing arts and politics, including members of Congress.

It is worth noting, of course, that over the same period the British signals intelligence agency, GCHQ, has conducted – without quite such lavish technical support – a very similar operation monitoring telegram traffic in Britain. Details were exposed in the *Daily Express* and *Daily Sketch* during 1967.

The British connection
The histories of Menwith Hill, Hunters Stones and the NSA itself have been closely – if very privately – interwined for 25 years. NSA was formed in 1952, and ordered to monitor foreign communications under a top secret and still classified directive called NSCID-6. In October 1952, NSA took control of the interception operations of the US armed forces, including ASA and the US Air Force Security Service, which had just started two bases at Chicksands, near Bedford, and Kirknewton, a few miles west of Edinburgh.

Recently declassified files in the United States National Archives indicate that a critical and secret meeting to plan Anglo-American communications and electronic activities was due to take place two years later, between two civil service committees. These were the British Joint Communications Electronics Board (part of the Cabinet Office), and its US equivalent. Declassified correspondence shows that the NSA's forerunner, the ASA, was involved in this planning.

The meeting was scheduled for 11 October 1954, but no record of the actual meeting or its agenda can now be found in the archives. Inquiries of official archivists have elicited a response that the meeting never, in the end, took place as 'joint objectives had already been agreed'.

By the end of October 1954, War Office surveyors were on site at Menwith Hill. The Post Office simultaneously began plans for its 'Backbone' microwave tower chain, and these were described in the February 1955 White Paper:

The Post Office are planning . . . a special network both by cable and by radio, designed to maintain long distance communication in the event of attack.

This was largely misleading flannel. In April 1955, local MP James Ramsden was told that the Menwith Hill site was to become a 'US Army radio station'. Construction began in April 1956 and an initial seven US army personnel set up on 1 May 1956. The following year, it was retitled the 13th US Army Security Agency Field Station. But then nothing happened until June 1959.

Precisely the same delays afflicted the Post Office's plans, which were first laid in detail during 1955. We have obtained 'confidential' copies of most of these early plans, which were supplied by the Post Office at the time to the Council for the Preservation of Rural England (CPRE). A detailed map, dated June 1956, shows a chain of 14 towers running roughly from London to Carlisle, via Manchester and Birmingham. The new stations would provide Britain with its first long distance radio microwave network – until then, such systems had only been used in an isolated and *ad hoc* way for carrying television.

The Hunters Stones network

The 1956 plan and subsequent developments show that the Hunters Stones tower was, unacknowledged, at the centre of the system. This emerges in various ways:

● The Post Office had already built a microwave system from Manchester to Scotland, which ran through Leeds. But when the new system was built, it was routed also through an additional and technically wholly unnecessary tower just ten miles from Leeds, at Hunters Stones.

● The Hunters Stones tower came under intense environmental pressure, like many others. The Post Office shifted the two towers just north of Hunters Stones and the one immediately south, back to

Brady C.J., 17 Dr... ... .rau...ugate 07636
Brady D.A, 17 Castle Clo,Killinghall ....Harrogate 56467
Brady E, 10 Roseville Rd.............................Harrogate 884245
Brady John, 18 Park House Gn ....Harrogate 55941
Brady L.G, 14 Greenfields Dv ....Harrogate 887810
Brady P.J, 9 Deep Ghyll Croft..........................Ripon 5678
Braeuninger A.D, 111 Menwith Hill Stn ....Harrogate 770912
Brailsford F, 159 Otley Rd ....Harrogate 69051
Braim Paul, 11 Dale Clo,Hampsthwaite...........Harrogate 7705'
Braime J.L, 7 York Pl,Knaresboro ....Harrogate 863⁵
Braime J.S, 33 Glebe Meadow,Sharow ....Ripo'
        26a West Park ....Harro⁣⁣
          " A⁣⁣   ⁣⁣

Albert Dale Braeuninger was the Chief of NSA's Menwith Hill Station until late 1980. Although he claimed to work for the US Department of Defense, his name does not appear in any of the last 25 years DoD directories. Above: Harrogate telephone directory listing.

existing sites. But they refused to move the new site at Hunters Stones.

● Resiting the other towers meant that Hunters Stones would have to be built a costly 200 feet taller to take special links. They still refused to move it.

● The system was eventually built through Hunters Stones as planned. Soon after, east-west links were added to the system, running to York and Lancaster. Four separate links then joined up at Hunters Stones.

Late in 1956, everything came to a halt. Both Post Office and Menwith Hill plans went into suspended animation until early in 1959. In the meantime, the Post Office dried up; a letter to CPRE, in December 1956, refers to 'misgivings . . . we have been very closely examining the whole scheme again'.

The sudden silence is not difficult to explain. Anglo-American secret intelligence relationships had suffered their most serious fracture during the Suez invasion, and the US was accused in Parliament of cracking British military and diplomatic cyphers. It was small wonder that Menwith Hill went into abeyance.

A recently declassified NSA 'Telecommunications Support Plan' of May 1956 shows that Menwith Hill had by then been included in its worldwide listening operations. The plan gives details of a 'COMINT Communications Relay Centre' which was built at Chicksands, Bedfordshire. Chicksands was linked to NSA, GCHQ, Kirknewton, and other British and American listening stations and headquarters.

Post Office plans were reactivated during 1959, and construction of the Backbone chain began early in 1960. Menwith Hill began to build up to strength; 32 new personnel arrived to start operations during June 1959, and the station officially opened fifteen months later. It eventually had an authorised staff of 506. By 1961, construction costs had exceeded $6 million.

Because of environmental difficulties, Hunters' Stones was completed later than other towers, during the winter of 1961, and was commissioned in 1962. At first, a cable was laid direct to the base, in a cross-country ditch. Using the CPRE files, and several years prior research on the contemporary Post Office tower network, it is possible to portray the subsequent development of the network that fed Hunters Stones:

● The first link went south from Harrogate to London. But soon after a special new route bypassed London and finished up at a tower at Fairseat, near Maidstone.

● A Ministry of Works surveyor in June 1962 inadvertently sent the CPRE a letter showing that the radio links from Fairseat would go three ways: London, Paris and Harrogate. The third connection from Fairseat – across England to Hunters Stones – could play no sensible part in a communications circuit between London and Paris. Nor, evidently, are Harrogate and Maidstone such centres of commercial activity as to merit their own hot-line. The surveyor's letter showed clearly that the northward link was to be installed simultaneously as part of the *London-Paris* connection. It could only be a tap.

● In 1963, new links were added: east to a tower at The Stonebow in the centre of York; west, to Quernmore near Lancaster; and north to Craigowl Hill near Dundee.

● The claim that the new system was for use 'in the event of attack' was untrue. Such a system, linking radar stations and control centres, was built by the Post Office and added to the microwave network. But it was designed and built two years *after* the other links. It follows different routes.

● Since 1963, other connections have been fed into Hunters' Stones. One line branches off from near Oxford towards Plymouth. Currently, there are two other connections which stop at Hunters Stones; from Manchester, and from London.

Scooping up new links abroad

A map published by the Post Office in 1973 provides a quantitative measure of Menwith Hill's capacity. The map shows that the four original links had each a capacity for 3,600 simultaneous telephone calls in and out. This gives a total of 14,400 lines.

But the *International Frequency List,* a voluminous international directory compiled in Geneva, contains additional information. The entries in the 1979 list based entirely on information supplied by the Post Office

NSA Headquarters, Fort George G Meade, near Washington DC.

itself, show that Hunters Stones besides relaying roughly 10,000 ordinary telephone calls, several TV channels, and data from northern early warning radar stations, has additional connections. According to this official source 5,400 additional *inward only* circuits feed into Hunters Stones, mostly from Leeds, and ultimately London.

The link to London has access to the international exchanges, and thus the whole panoply of international connections. The link to York is well placed to connect to submarine cables to Scandinavia and north west Europe, some of which leave from Scarborough. The link to Lancaster can access transatlantic cables, and connections to Ireland.

Although every section of the Menwith Hill network cannot be exactly traced, its purpose is clear. As the international communications network has boomed over the past three decades, Menwith Hill has been able to scoop up each new link abroad.

The critical phase came in 1966 when NSA took over. A USAF unit at Kirknewton (the 6952nd Radio Squadron Mobile) and the ASA Field Station closed on the same day – 1 August 1966. The change had been anticipated; the local paper printed a report that civilians were to take over during January 1966. US spokesmen said the story was untrue. But by July 70 NSA personnel were esconced in Harrogate's Grand Hotel, and the takeover had begun. Personnel and tasks were transferred from Kirknewton down to Harrogate.

One of the Kirknewton analysts who left USAFSS before the move south was a young conscript to the USAF. Jim Haynes is well known in British arts circles for his role in starting the Edinburgh Traverse Theatre, the London Arts Lab, and the *International Times* (IT). He is not well known for having worked for NSA when he first came to Scotland. He told us about Kirknewton's tasks:

I monitored commercial telegram networks . . . between London,
Paris, Moscow, Beograd, Cairo . . . Machines in intercept rooms,
tuned to transmission channels, would spew out 8-ply paper. I worked
on one of the plies . . .

Watch lists were used at Kirknewton. Many of the items looked for
concerned commodities or financial information.

Since the early '60s, communications have increasingly been sent by
cable or satellite. Thus centres for radio monitoring like Kirknewton have
become outdated. In contrast, Menwith Hill's taps on international links
provided the ideal input from cables instead.

By last year, international communications to and from Britain had
built up to considerable proportions, including 13 million telegrams and
184 million telephone calls – some merely 'transiting' through Britain.

But such vast volumes are well within NSA's reach. In 1974 alone,
according to the Church Committee report and other sources, NSA's
HARVEST facility and others like it were, in the US alone, sifting through
75 million telegrams in one year – 1.8 million were then sorted out for
subsequent human analysis. The information gained is processed according
to the requirements of Key Intelligence Questions which are political,
military and economic. Commercial intelligence, after being 'sanitised', is
available to large US corporations through NSA Special Security Officers
attached to the companies. Much the same happens at GCHQ in Britain.

The Pike Committee report gave a useful insight into the commercial
targets of US monitoring; they found:

at least one new area of non-political and non military emphasis in
international intercept – economic intelligence. Communications
interception in this area has developed rapidly since 1972, partly in
reaction to the Arab oil embargo and the failure to obtain good
information on Russian grain production and negotiations for purchase
with American corporations.

Once again Menwith Hill, straddling the main US communications routes
to Eastern Europe and the Middle East, is NSA's prime source.

Menwith Hill, according to a former British military officer and
several other locally employed personnel, went on high alert at unusual
times. One such occasion was when the NSA's spy ship *Pueblo* was
captured off North Korea. More interestingly, however, all say that the base
works overtime immediately *after* an IRA bomb incident or other terrorist
activity in Britain.

The timing is revealing. It is not the base guards who go on overtime.
The agents' job, one official who has worked with NSA explained in
Washington, is to sift through *already recorded* communications to find a
message between Britain and Ireland and elsewhere concerning the
forthcoming attack. 'Tape is cheap', the official explained, 'storing an hour's
calls on a 1,000 line link is simple' and would use less than $100 worth of
tape.

The Hunters Stones tower has direct microwave links to other towers at Lancaster and Manchester which, between them could provide access to all the lines between Britain and Ireland, as well as many transatlantic circuits. Such taps would also facilitate keeping watch after an explosion, in case of further communication by returning bombers. The inclusion of the terrorists and their ilk as NSA targets may be an inexpensive gesture made to the British government for the extraordinary facility that the Post Office has provided for NSA to spy on British communications.

'No comment'
This account of Menwith Hill's operations has been put, in some detail, to the Post Office, the Ministry of Defence, NSA base Chief Braueninger, NSA itself, and its Special US Liaison Officer, who is former NSA Deputy Director Benson Buffham (now billed as a 'Political Attache' at the US Embassy).

NSA would only say that its British operation was classified, and this covered any computers there. The Post Office has had equally little to say. Albert Dale Braeuninger, Menwith Hill Chief, was initially quite forthcoming on what he claimed the base didn't do; suggestions that they monitored national and international communications were, he said 'rubbish'. Pressed for a specific explanation of its facilities, however, he resorted to waffle:

We do radio-relays [a standard euphemism for sigint] – material comes in from a variety of places and is rerouted. It is a switching operation. We route it sometimes to the UK and sometimes to the US.

Although he made Menwith Hill sound like a central London exchange, the above description scarcely refutes our relevations. Asked specifically about NSA, he retreated:

It is not pertinent for me to discuss our organisational relationships within the UK or outside. You cannot really expect me to answer what kind of work goes on here either in a technical or operational sense.

When these and similar questions were repeated to the NSA office in London last week, and also to the Ministry of Defence, they too retreated behind familiar covers. Menwith Hill, they said, is a 'communications relay centre for the (US) Department of Defence.'

We then resubmitted detailed questions to the Ministry of Defence and the American Embassy, and asked for interviews. We also asked the Home Office and the Foreign Office if they had issued any warrants for the interception of international communications. No information was forthcoming from any of them. Whitehall, it appears, is ready to join in protecting NSA from British as well as American inspection.

First published 18 July 1980

POSTSCRIPT

Postscript 1: NSA spies on British government

The British government is one of the targets of the US National Security Agency communications monitoring operations, despite the remarkable facility with which Britain has provided it at Menwith Hill. In fact, according to published sources and a US intelligence consultant, Menwith – together with other sites in the US, Germany and Italy – is a centre for 'Project Wideband Extraction'. One of the products of wideband extraction, which emerges from banks of machines at the US Army Security Agency's interception station at Vint Hill Farms, near Warrington, Virginia, is the British government's communications around the world.

This was revealed in a secret 1975 congressional report; the Fink Report to the House Committee on Government Operations and Individual Rights, then led by Congresswoman Bella Abzug. A study of NSA reported that:

> NSA monitors the traffic of specific countries, including Great Britain, our closest ally. The monitoring of government traffic has been confirmed by a former employee of Vint Hill Farms station. (The station) had a whole bank of machines (and) a whole team of men whose only job was to read and process intercepted British communications.

Paradoxically, the 'secret' Fink report containing these references was published, unattributed and unnoticed, during 1978 hearings on the US's new Foreign Intelligence Surveillance Act.

Project Wideband Extraction, with which Menwith Hill and other NSA stations are connected, started operations at the Vint Hill Farm station during July 1969. The job, as the name implies, was to extract signals and messages of intelligence interest from a 'wideband' containing hundreds of thousands of other communications. Sometimes these communications would be transmitted around the world by satellite for analysis, after being intercepted. More often, according to US intelligence officials, giant freight aircraft would fly back to the US from Europe and Australia, loaded with reels of magnetic tape to feed into analysing computers.

Menwith Hill carries out a great deal of wideband interception and extraction. References to another site for 'wideband' work have also appeared in unclassified US defence appropriations hearings. This is at Gablingen, near Augsberg in Germany, which is the headquarters of the US Army Security Agency's 502d Group, responsible for interception throughout Germany.

Augsburg's role in telephone tapping was inadvertently confirmed by Pentagon lawyers in two recent civil rights cases. An army officer and some US civilians living in Germany had sued the US Defense Department for unlawful spying on their activities. During the course of the case, the Pentagon produced a short list of units which had the capacity to tap or bug telephone calls in Germany. The 502d ASA Group at Augsburg was included. (In a recent reorganisation the US Army Security Agency has become the Intelligence and Security Command, and Augsburg has become the 66th Intelligence and Security Group HQ.)

According to two former US intelligence officials, the sites of US tapping operations in Germany are Berlin (where the allied powers can freely tap any phones they like) and Baumholder. The Baumholder station was consolidated in 1972 with all other Army Security Agency operations at Augsburg. Another minor tapping site is in Italy, where NSA is known to have two bases, at Treviso and Brindisi. Some of the submarine cables which cross the Mediterranean basin to the Near and Middle East can only be reached in this area.

Another site for tapping international phone and telex calls was in Sidi Yahia, near Rabat in Morocco. This base mostly intercepted French signals and cables. It has now closed and moved to Rota in southern Spain. A former analyst for NSA's Naval Security Group, who worked for more than a year at Sidi Yahia, described its operations to us:

> In one eight hour shift you would go through perhaps 500-600 pages of telex type sheets . . . Once a week I was asked to translate a telephone tap tape . . .

He had to watch for and file references to such people as Stokely Carmichael, Robert Mugabe, Holden Roberto, Frelimo . . . 'and any British or American diplomats in the area'.

The headquarters of Project Wideband has now been moved to a giant new 'Central Security Operations Station', which NSA has set up at San Antonio, Texas. Over 5,000 servicemen and NSA personnel work full time on analysing intercepts from around the world.

First published 25 July 1980

John Vernon Mills, base security officer, ill-temperedly hung around TV crews who filmed Menwith Hill after the *New Statesman* revelations. He told the BBC that he 'didn't wish to dignify the article with a comment'.

Postscript 2: No official denial

Despite some confused reports to the contrary, no British or American government department denied the allegations in the *New Statesman* on 18 July 1980 that the US National Security Agency's Menwith Hill Station in Yorkshire is conducting mass tapping of international telephone and telegraph messages.

The Ministry of Defence – the only department prepared to deal with the issue – issued only what a spokesman termed a 'curiously specific' and highly 'limited' denial; namely that Menwith Hill was not intercepting translantic incoming or outgoing calls, nor was it listening to any domestic calls in the UK.

The accuracy of official comments on communications interception has not, historically, been reliable. But in any case, the Ministry's comments are virtually a tacit acknowledgement that Menwith Hill can listen in, as we described, to all calls to Europe, transatlantic calls going

Spooks' Party: NSA agents from Menwith Hill celebrate at a showing of the film *Yanks* at a local Harrogate cinema.

through Britain, and all telex and telegram traffic. As Bob Cryer MP suggested to the House of Commons after the allegations were published, the pronouncement (by the Leader of the House of Commons, Norman St John Stevas) that no minister was prepared to comment conceded their accuracy by default.

The Post Office claimed – quite wrongly – that all aspects of interception were covered in the April Home Office White Paper. But they did lift the shutters a little. They now admit to running the high capacity cable that feeds Menwith Hill. But it's a 'private circuit' – and they can't talk about it.

First published 25 July 1980